ITA Nashville
May 1986

THE
EMBOUCHURE

TO
DANY

THE
EMBOUCHURE

by

MAURICE M. PORTER

LONDON

BOOSEY AND HAWKES

FOREWORD

by

FRANK WRIGHT, M.B.E., F.G.S.M., L.R.S.M. (Lond.), Hon. F.T.C.L.

For many years now the name of Maurice M. Porter has been well known among wind musicians throughout this country and beyond.

Articles from his pen have appeared from time to time in a number of authoritative publications, including *Grove's Dictionary of Music & Musicians*. His help and opinion have been sought by amateur and professional wind musicians alike, among them some of the finest in the world. He has spoken at important gatherings of players, and lectured at postgraduate university level. One of his earlier talks in particular created uncommon interest—that given at the Annual Convention of the National Association of Brass Band Conductors at the Guildhall School of Music and Drama, London, some twelve years ago. This was subsequently reproduced in the Association's official journal, *The Conductor* and later in the Besson publication *Brass Today*.

Mr. Porter's main theme has always remained constant—"The Embouchure and its Problems," a subject of which he has made almost a life study.

To say that a book by Mr. Porter on this subject is long overdue is no mere glib statement; it is simply the truth. The absence of such material, so highly relevant to wind instrument playing, alone stresses its need. It is doubtful whether anything quite like this book has appeared before. Mr. Porter has delved deep into his subject with a combination of natural enthusiasm and a profound anatomical knowledge of the Embouchure Musculature. Just how wide has been his research a glance at the following chapters will show.

"The Embouchure" will prove a valuable book to all teachers and students of wind instruments. Not only will it be helpful to those who on occasions have anxious thoughts about their embouchure—"my lip doesn't feel too good" is almost a common-place remark heard among wind players—but its intelligent study will also provide a store of fascinating information and go a long way towards lifting the veil on "how it all works".

PREFACE

The subject of the Embouchure is by no means simple. It is in fact very complex. The more I studied it over the years, the more it disclosed fields for further research. Numerous articles on the subject have appeared both here and abroad in a multitude of journals. Some have been not only controversial but quite inaccurate. The reason for this is easy to understand. A student of an instrument of music must be dedicated to his work if he is to attain any degree of success. And should he hope to become a "wind" musician, he would surely find little enough time to learn the fundamentals—still less the details—of the anatomy and physiology he applies to the playing of his instrument. To acquire such knowledge would itself require intense study for some years. It is, therefore, small wonder that from time to time one comes across articles in journals or chapters in books on wind instrument playing that are a long way from anatomical and physiological fact. These also reveal a variety of opinions, some of which are scientifically absurd.

Unquestionably, the embouchure is of vital importance to all wind musicians; and many besides myself have for a long time been convinced that a book on the subject, the purpose of which would be to answer the many questions on musculature, to describe, as far as possible, the variations in different players and to help solve the numerous problems in individuals, is long overdue.

Should any of the text seem to some readers unduly complicated and technical, I would remind them that anatomy and physiology are complicated and technical subjects inevitably embracing, one might add, the embouchure apparatus itself! Most readers, I think, will find the book intelligible and, I hope, enlightening generally and helpful individually; and if I succeed in stimulating further thought, or even research, so much the better for wind musicians everywhere.

ACKNOWLEDGMENTS

It gives me much pleasure to record my sincere gratitude to the many musical friends, scientists, and others who offered me help and encouragement in the work of preparing this book. Among them are Mr. Frank Wright and Mr. Eric McGavin, who were most enthusiastic about my writing a book on Embouchure. They offered me much valuable advice and many useful suggestions throughout and to them I am deeply indebted.

My thanks are due to the Managing Director, Mr. David Adams, and the staff of the Publications Department of Messrs. Boosey and Hawkes, who have given me all the help they could. I am particularly grateful to Mr. Herbert N. Lemon and Mr. Stanley Smeed for their practical aid in guiding the manuscript into print. To Mr. Leslie J. Godden, the Editor of *The British Dental Journal*, I owe my sincere appreciation for his many kindnesses and helpful suggestions; I also extend to him and the publishers of that journal my grateful thanks for their courtesy in allowing me to use several of the illustrations from my earlier articles on the Embouchure. My thanks are also due to Mrs. Joyce Harris for her secretarial assistance with the manuscript, to Mr. Stuart Smith for helping me with reading the proofs, and to the artists Mr. Patrick Kemmish, Miss Sylvia Treadgold, Mr. Richard Harrison and Mr. Antony Ososki for their help with the illustrations.

Research and the preparation of the text had continued intermittently for some years, during which time I was leading a very busy professional life. I did, however, avail myself of the opportunities, when they arose, of communicating either personally or by letter with the following, whose help in various ways I most gratefully acknowledge: Sir Thomas Armstrong, Mr. Philip Bate, the late Mr. Eric Blom, Dr. A. Bouhuys, Dr. W. D. W. Brooks, Mr. Jack Brymer, Dr. E. J. M. Campbell, Miss Janet Craxton,

Mr. Stanley Creber, Mr. Leslie Evans, Mr. Ernest Hall, the late Mr. Max Hinrichsen, Mr. Reginald Kell, Miss Thea King, Mr. Lyndesay G. Langwill, Mr. Jack Mackintosh, Mr. Brian Manton-Myatt, Mr. Patrick O'Keefe, Mrs. Adrienne Phillips, Dr. Anna Roche, Mr. Arnold Rose, Dr. Gerald Russell, Miss E. Muriel Spencer, the late Mr. Frederick J. Thurston and the late Mr. Bryan J. Wood.

Finally, I am deeply grateful to the directors of the following institutions for the use of the libraries, museums and other departments: The Royal Society of Medicine; The Royal College of Surgeons of England; The British Dental Association; The Periodontal Department of the Eastman Dental Hospital, London; The Periodontal Department of Tufts University, Boston, Mass.; The Royal Academy of Music; The Royal College of Music; and the Royal Military School of Music, Kneller Hall.

M.M.P.

CONTENTS

CONTENTS

INTRODUCTION

The purpose of this book is to convey to wind musicians and to all others concerned the conclusions of a long research into the make-up of the embouchure. In addition to describing its musculature and the architecture of the more important structures involved, the book is intended to provide examples of the subtle influences which could disturb the musician's embouchure and to suggest how these influences can be eliminated or avoided. I have also tried to relate the embouchure to certain phenomena during playing, such as resonance and fatigue, and to suggest ways of maintaining the developed embouchure for as long as possible.

It is apparent that to attain the status of a first-class wind musician, according to present-day standards, is to achieve something high indeed. Some modern composers, one is told, seem to have taken for granted the high standard of technical ability of the present-day wind musician to the extent that they expect him, on occasions, to play passages that are well-nigh impossible. Moreover, they expect him to play them with an appropriate grace and facility. Doubtless, there are many wind musicians able to play such passages flawlessly from a technical point of view and with splendid musicianship. To these attributes add yet another— a tone of rare quality, and here you surely have the great artist. One is prompted to ask why relatively few players are able to cultivate the fine quality of tone which at once elevates them above the rest. An attempt to answer this question involves one immediately in the riddle of the individual embouchure. However fluent a wind player becomes and however competent he might be in such matters as phrasing and breath control, it is in the quality of his tone, or the very sounds he produces, that he will be mainly judged.

Most players will know that tone quality depends not only on the instrument and mouthpiece—the intelligent musician will spare no effort or expense to find both instrument and mouthpiece best suited to him—but also, and the importance of this can hardly be overstressed, on the embouchure of the player. On one occasion the author was quite shocked to hear the comments of a

1

well-known music critic concerning the playing of a very experienced wind soloist in a concerto. "That man has a truly remarkable technique," he said, "but it pains me to hear the sounds he emits. At best, they are mediocre." That such a conflict of abilities can exist in the one player is astonishing and sad; it surely points to one thing—a faulty or disturbed embouchure. Not infrequently a student may have felt, or been advised, that his embouchure was "not quite right". He may also have heard of others being blessed by nature with the "perfect" embouchure. That some players are endowed from the start with splendid natural embouchures there is no doubt. But this does not mean that good embouchures cannot be cultivated in others. The near-perfect embouchure involves the co-ordination of many factors, and what is considered even the best in many players could probably be improved, given time and expert advice.

Any embouchure, even the near-perfect one, can be disturbed by abrupt or slow changes within the mouth. A good example is the case of the mature player with a sharp corner of a tooth which annoys his lip. This forces him to adopt an embouchure requiring much more effort in co-ordinating and controlling the muscles than when the tooth is smoothed or otherwise corrected.

But there are many more conditions other than the sharp corner of a tooth which can interfere with the development and maintenance of a fine embouchure. Some of these insidiously compel the player to produce, habitually, a sound decidedly lacking in attraction.

Every serious musician, I am told, must know that although there are many good ways of learning to play an instrument at all well, so far as technique is concerned, all these methods are devoted to achieving the same end. Certain fundamentals, such as scales and exercises, must be practised thoroughly in order to become proficient. There are not many short cuts. What appear to be short cuts are really only more concise methods of learning aimed at eliminating waste of valuable time. Here, the good teacher's words of advice can be invaluable. Should the student ignore or by-pass some of these fundamentals, he does so at his own peril, since his playing will inevitably be weak in some important respects. A similar approach could apply to the study of the embouchure. The more thoroughly it is understood, the more it will be appreciated what factors enable a player to acquire a high quality of tone and tone colour. It is then more likely that the player might find means to improve his own embouchure.

Here, then, is a compendium of the results of my own approach and research into the complex subject of embouchure which, it is hoped, will enable the wind musician to understand some of the vital facts about his own playing and that of his pupils. Together with the experience he has already acquired, it might enable him to achieve that high quality of tone, so essential to a first-class musician; or it might enable him to "produce", "nurse" and "develop" from among his pupils the most successful and sought-after players. With the aid of the glossary of anatomical terms at the back of the book the reader should have little difficulty in following the more technical details. The first chapter gives my definition of embouchure which should satisfy scientific as well as musical requirements. It also includes an outline of gross functions of the jaws, lips, teeth, tongue, and other organs in the blowing of wind instruments generally.

Hitherto, there appears to have been a generally accepted distinction between "technique" and "tone" in playing a musical instrument. For teaching and other purposes this seemed to have a definite advantage, since the pupil was made aware immediately where he was at fault when his playing was under scrutiny by his professor or a critic. For example, he regarded faulty technique as faulty "fingering," with, possibly, errors in phrasing, articulation, and so on. But he distinguished this from the "tone", "tone-colour", the "quality" of sound, that he was capable of producing.

Latterly, however, "technique" has been described in some quarters, and by at least one authority[1], as the total effect of a musician's or pupil's playing. There may be some very good and admirable purpose in this in order to train the musician, particularly the advanced one, to achieve a unified near-perfect "whole" as in the soloist or artist. However, since this book is mainly concerned with the embouchure and because this deals mostly with sound production, tone-colour, articulation, their control and problems in playing, it has been considered wiser to refer to "technique" in this book as "fingering" and ability to achieve

3

the exact notes at the precise time required by the music. Therefore, except where otherwise stated, "tone" will be regarded as the sound effect the player is able to produce by coupling his own embouchure with his instrument.

The professor's or teacher's advice is frequently sought on the student's choice of a wind instrument. His opinion might also be relied upon when, on certain occasions, he could be sitting on audition boards or panels, interviewing or examining candidates. In such circumstances his ability to assess *embouchure potential* would be a valuable asset. Too often later reflection on his decision, already given, leaves him in some doubt as to whether he gave the right one. The chapter on "Embouchure Potential" should go a fair way in helping him out of his dilemma. Before giving a considered opinion he could take into account the conditions possibly present in the candidate hindering an embouchure of comfort. Such conditions are discussed in the chapter on "Embouchure Comfort and Discomfort". The chapter on the embouchure in relation to staccato includes a fairly detailed description of the tongue, since this organ is so vitally concerned with articulation in the playing of all wind instruments[2]. In some players the tongue is a tantalising organ to control at speed in staccato playing and since "tip-control" may not be possible in some (even after many years of practice), the author has classified "tip-tonguing", "dorsal-tonguing" (or "top-tonguing") and "pharyngeal-tonguing" (or "back-tonguing") for discretional use by teachers in helping students.

The chapter on the "Embouchure in Relation to Legato" stresses the rôle of the embouchure musculature and tongue in controlling the air column. It also stresses the need for adequate recognition, by composer and conductor, of the value of rest periods to the wind musician, so that he may be free from unnecessary strain.

In the chapter on the "Embouchure and Breathing" difficulty had been encountered in deciding just how much scientific detail should be included in a book of this nature intended for wind musicians. Teachers of wind instruments often advocate their own methods of breathing and in so doing become involved in such subjects as the respiratory muscles and the mechanics of breathing. These demand not only some knowledge of anatomy and physiology, but a scientist's approach to a highly specialised and detailed study of the subject, which, it is considered, is beyond the scope of a work of this kind. Should the reader, however, require authoritative physiological information of this character, in the light of modern knowledge, he is referred to such outstanding work as that of Dr. E. J. Moran Campbell.[3] In addition to objective discussions on the action of the muscles of respiration, it also includes such valuable scientific studies as the use and interpretation of the Pressure Volume Diagram. This and other valuable scientific works are listed, for those readers interested, in the index of references at the back of the book.

There is no doubt that oral hygiene is of great importance to the community as a whole in the prevention of many diseases.[4] Therefore, it is only logical that for the professional wind musician the maintenance of a high standard of oral hygiene is vital for his career. It is for this reason that the chapters on "Care of the Embouchure" and "Cleanliness of Instrument" are considered too important to omit. Since "tartar" is responsible, either directly or indirectly, for so much gum trouble, pyorrhœa and loosening or loss of the teeth[5], an account is given of its accumulation around the teeth, the saliva from which it is normally deposited and the glands from which the saliva is secreted. Also discussed is the ever present scourge of dental caries (decay), neglect of which can almost ruin a potentially excellent embouchure.

Accumulations of both tartar, which can result in gum trouble, and of food debris, which can result in caries[6], both require the meticulous attention of the wind musician if his embouchure is to remain unimpaired for a very long time. I have, therefore, described a systematic yet simple method of cleaning the teeth in the chapter on "Care of the Embouchure".

"Embouchure Aids" is a subject which has interested me for many years. And I have included a separate chapter on this subject of which the purpose is to encourage wind musicians whose careers may be plagued by embouchure troubles arising from accident or disease. In these cases very real help can often be given by the dental profession. This chapter could be regarded as a small tribute to dental surgeons whose efforts on behalf of their patients are so seldom lauded or, in some cases, even appreciated.

Introduction

I have considered the muscles closely associated with the embouchure, i.e., of the face, mouth, tongue, chest, diaphragm and abdomen, in what I think is sufficient substance and detail to interest the wind musician, professor or teacher. One could go into far more anatomy and anatomical detail involving a host of other muscles in the body and their functions, for example those concerned with the excursions of the lower jaw, with the neck, upper limb, back (e.g., in posture), and so on. However, I make no excuse for not doing so. The result would have been not only an unwieldy anatomical text book, but an added applied treatise in so far as it concerns the wind musician, both of which would have made the book bulkier by several hundreds of pages. Such, obviously, was not the intention. For too long the embouchure has been a controversial subject and it was to try to clear up much of this controversy by exposing as many of the obscure facts as possible that I was prompted to devote the time necessary to the writing of this book and the research which it involved.

THE EMBOUCHURE—THEORY AND FACT*

The word "Embouchure" is French in origin. Literally, it means "opening into"; musically, it is referred to in wind instrument playing to indicate the "mode of applying the lips to a wind instrument". The equivalent term in German is "Ansetzen", the literal meaning of which is "setting-on". Another German term, "Einsetzen" has been referred to in the playing of the horn,[7] where the mouthpiece appeared to be set inside the lower lip. The literal meaning of Einsetzen is "setting-in". For the purposes of this book I will define the embouchure as:

> The mode of applying the lips and mouth to the mouthpiece of a wind instrument as expertly advised and the mode actually adopted or developed by a player for a particular mouthpiece of a wind instrument.

LIPS AND MOUTH WOULD INVOLVE:

(a) Muscles: Orbicularis oris and the muscles which radiate from it.

(b) Tongue: Intrinsic and extrinsic muscles.

(c) Teeth: Mainly the maxillary and mandibular anterior teeth.

(d) Maxillæ: As well as other bones of the head and neck to which embouchure muscles are attached.

(e) The palate, pharynx and air sinuses of the face and head which play a part.

MOUTHPIECE WOULD IMPLY:

(a) Mouthpiece alone—in the case of all brass instruments and the flute and piccolo.

(b) Mouthpiece plus Reed—in the case of the single reed instruments, e.g., clarinet, saxophone.

(c) Reed alone—in the case of the double reed instruments, e.g., oboe, cor anglais, bassoon.

These differing types of mouthpiece could be a convenient

---

*A glossary of medical and other technical terms used in the text is provided at the back of the book.

means of classifying wind instruments for those dealing with embouchure defects, such as doctors or dentists. By analogy the gross functions of the more important organs involved in blowing any wind instrument could be described as follows:

The *Lungs*, assisted by a plunger, the *Diaphragm*, act as bellows and furnish the supply of air to the mouth. The *Mouth* in turn acts as a funnel-reservoir in guiding the current of air through the instrument. Together with the instrument, it gives "shape" and "body" to the sound emitted. It also, together with certain cavities of the head and neck, has a profound effect on resonance through the instrument; the air sinuses warm and moisten the air to assist blowing.

The part played by the *Tongue* is similar to that of a valve, whether it directly damps the vibrations of the reed or lips (acting as the reed in brass) by contact, or whether it disconnects the flow of air by touching the palate or the back of the front upper teeth or the lips.

The *Lips* have a similar function to that of a washer in reed instruments and the dual function of washer and reed in brass instruments. In the latter case, the portions of the lips within the cup of the mouthpiece act as reed and vibrate; the portions of the lips against the rim of the mouthpiece act as a washer, preventing the escape of air while playing. The flute requires an adaptation of the lips totally different from that of reed instruments or brass. In this case, the "modiolus" (see below), just behind the angles of the mouth, is made more tense in a lateral direction by the increased contraction of the risorius (smiling) and buccinator muscles (see Figs. 1 and 2). This permits the free margin of the lips, surrounding the column of expired air directed across the hole in the instrument, to exert delicate control on the sound generator. The rest of the lips (orbicularis oris muscle—Fig. 1) and the modiolus take on a washer-like function to prevent or minimize the escape of air through the sides of the mouth.

The *Teeth* and *Jaws* form the girders and scaffolding respectively which support the lips, mouth and tongue, i.e., the whole of the embouchure musculature.

Viewed from the front, the embouchure musculature of both sides of the mouth may be looked upon as the convex surface of an open umbrella with the ferrule end of the cane removed so as to leave a small opening, analogous to the aperture of the mouth. In brass instrument and flute playing the mouthpiece is outside the mouth (extra-oral), while all reed instruments are played with the mouthpiece inside the mouth (intra-oral). Fig. 1 shows diagrammatically the scheme of muscles involved. These are numbered clockwise on each side of the mouth around a small knotty area near the angle. This area is known as the *modiolus*[8] (a name, although a highly specialised anatomical one, which wind musicians are likely to notice more frequently in future literature on the embouchure). Modiolus means, literally, the nave or hub of a wheel. The spokes of the wheel are represented by all the other muscles of the embouchure which radiate from it *on each side of the mouth.*

Just as we have two arms, two eyes, two ears, so the modiolus and muscles radiating from it are on each side of the mouth. It is of importance to recognise it in this way, because certain conditions can arise which result in the modiolus and the muscles radiating from it on one side being thrown out of gear. This then

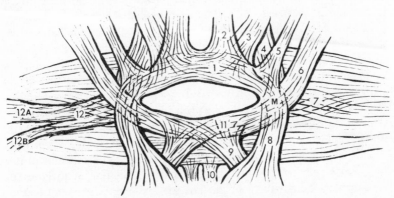

Fig. 1—Scheme of musculature of embouchure. (*Front view*)

1. Orbicularis oris (upper lip portion); 2. Levator labii superioris alæque nasi; 3. Levator labii superioris; 4. Levator anguli oris; 5. Zygomaticus minor; 6. Zygomaticus major; 7. Buccinator; 8. Depressor anguli oris; 9. Depressor labii inferioris; 10. Mentalis; 11. Orbicularis oris (lower lip portion); 12. Risorius; 12A Risorius (masseteric strand); 12B Risorius (platysma strand); M, Modiolus.

NOTE: The risorius muscle is removed on the subject's left side to show the decussating middle fibres of the buccinator muscle, which it would otherwise hide. The lower middle fibres of the buccinator go to the upper lip, whilst the upper middle fibres go to the lower lip.

needs a compensating effort by the modiolus and its muscles of the other side in order to restore the balance just as, in order to walk with a faulty leg, one adopts a limp which involves a compensating effort by the other leg to balance the body.

If one could imagine the embouchure musculature with the skin lifted like a veil from one side of the face, it would have an appearance as in Fig. 2. With the skin lifted from both sides, the appearance would be as in Fig. 3. For teaching purposes, Figs. 4, 5, 6, 7 and 8 show embouchure adaptation in the different classes of instrument, where the conditions of the jaws, face, mouth and teeth might be considered "within the bounds of the normal". These figures are in sagittal section.

The foremost teachers of wind instruments attempt to promote in their pupils the adoption of an embouchure of greatest comfort, consistent with the maximum efficiency in tone production. The relationship between individual teeth and between the lower jaw and the upper jaw can vary considerably among different players. For example, some persons have a protruding lower jaw (see Fig. 9), others have a receding lower jaw (with protruding upper teeth) (see Fig. 10). Any of these variations might create problems for the pupil and his teacher at the outset.[9] Some of these problems might be overcome but others might be too difficult for the particular instrument, so that the choice of another instrument might well be advised. A receding lower jaw with very prominent and protruding upper teeth, as in Fig. 10, can often be traced to continual mouth breathing caused by such conditions as adenoids, nasal obstruction,[10] the use of comforters, or excessive thumb-sucking in infancy (see Fig. 11). This often results in a poorly developed and insufficiently functional upper lip, which is very short. In this case it would be difficult to retain such a lip in a position covering the upper front teeth in order to play the oboe or bassoon, although some players manage to overcome the difficulty. Choice of instrument is therefore a matter of much importance to a student intending to become a professional wind musician. A student with a "normal" relationship between his upper and lower jaws and between his individual teeth has a considerable advantage at the outset on almost any instrument (see Fig. 12). It would be sad indeed, if a student's progress were limited in his future career because of embouchure

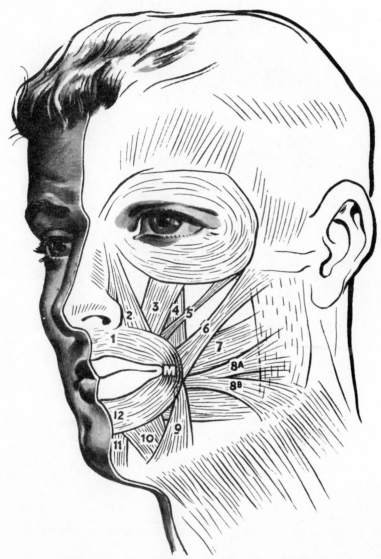

Fig. 2—Scheme of musculature of embouchure. (*Lateral view*)

1. Orbicularis oris (upper lip portion); 2. Levator labii superioris alæque nasi; 3. Levator labii superioris; 4. Levator anguli oris; 5. Zygomaticus minor; 6. Zygomaticus major; 7. Buccinator; 8A. Risorius (masseteric strand); 8B. Risorius (platysma strand); 9. Depressor anguli oris; 10. Depressor labii inferioris; 11. Mentalis; 12. Orbicularis oris (lower lip portion); M, Modiolus.

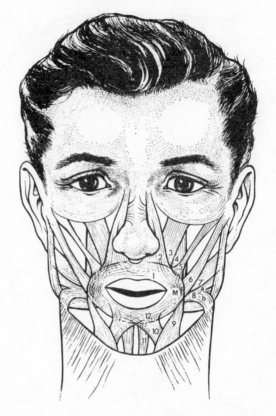

Fig. 3—Scheme of musculature of embouchure. (*Front view*)

1. Orbicularis oris (upper lip portion); 2. Levator labii superioris alæque nasi; 3. Levator labii superioris; 4. Levator anguli oris; 5. Zygomaticus minor; 6. Zygomaticus major; 7. Buccinator; 8A. Risorius (masseteric strand); 8B. Risorius (platysma strand); 9. Depressor anguli oris; 10. Depressor labii inferioris; 11. Mentalis; 12. Orbicularis oris (lower lip portion); M, Modiolus.

NOTE: The even contraction of these muscles on both sides to produce the "perfect" embouchure is rarely possible. Such an embouchure would demand perfect bone framework of the jaws and face, perfect girders (teeth) over which the embouchure muscles would be stretched, as well as perfect symmetry between both sides of the face. Innumerable minor conditions, permanent or temporary, could be present which prevent this, e.g., a space between teeth on one side (see Chapter III). However, by co-ordinating the contraction of the muscles of one side with the contraction of those of the other, a good compensating embouchure is possible.

Where the sides differ widely from each other, one modiolus with its muscles is strained heavily, whilst the other is more relaxed. The strained side tends to tire more easily. Practised co-ordination of the two sides help to control the defect. "Embouchure Aids" can assist considerably in some of these cases (see Chapter XI).

difficulties, no matter how good his musical background might be, or how great a desire he might have to play a particular instrument.

Where the teeth, lips and inter-relationship of the upper and lower jaws do not deviate too much from the "normal" and progress with the instrument is satisfactory, it would still be in the pupil's interest for the teacher not to be too insistent on the pupil holding his instrument in any preconceived "conventional" position if this is in any way going to hamper his breathing, embouchure or fingering. Frequently, with the best of intentions the teacher is unaware of the fact that he is unduly straining the pupil's neck or embouchure muscles. What he is easily able to do himself, so far as appearance of position of the instrument is concerned, might be an added strenuous effort for his pupil.

Types of face, lips, mouth, jaws and teeth are therefore matters the teacher might well consider, and often does, in training a pupil, no matter how intelligent and enthusiastic the pupil might be. Such considerations would seem to apply particularly to military or massed bands, where appearance of uniformity and smartness are accentuated. Where such uniformity must be insisted upon, an assessment of a candidate's potential in this respect could be made by a brief survey of not only lips, but jaw relationship and type of face. A dentist's report and models of the candidate's teeth and jaws would probably be a great help to the professor or teacher, especially where a choice of instrument has not yet been made (see Chapter III, page 47).

For the purpose of description a normality of conditions, or ideal, is often used. Such ideal conditions, however, rarely exist, particularly in the field of anatomy of the face. What does exist is a wide range of conditions which might be regarded as "within the bounds of the normal" (see Fig. 12). Since individuals vary considerably regarding their faces, jaws, etc., it would be more accurate for the purpose of description to speak of the theory of the embouchure and its musculature. It would be quite impossible to describe all its factual variations, but the general types of variation could be recognised by classifying a few of the possibilities later. Before proceeding to classify embouchure potential, it would be more appropriate and convenient to discuss the embouchure of comfort.

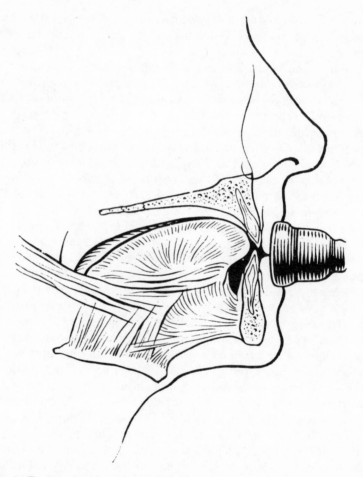

Fig. 4—To show the adaptation of the lips to the cup-like mouthpiece of the cornet or trumpet, where the jaws, face, mouth, teeth, etc., might be considered "within the bounds of the normal".

NOTE: The cup is covered half by the upper lip and half by the lower lip in most cases investigated. Some authorities, however, advocate two-thirds lower lip and one-third upper lip.

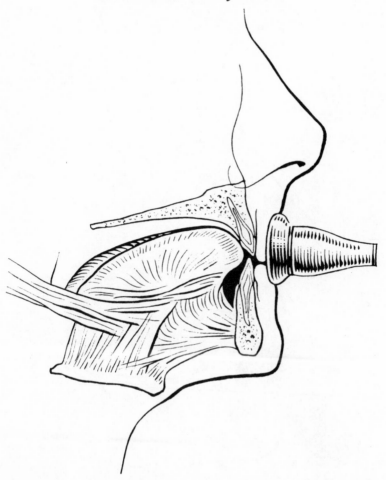

Fig. 5—To show the adaptation of the lips to the mouthpiece of the horn, where the jaws, face, mouth, teeth, etc., might be considered "within the bounds of the normal".

NOTE: (1) The mouthpiece is covered two-thirds by the upper and one-third by the lower lip. (2) Players of brass instruments with larger mouthpieces (trombone, tuba and such like) tend to use more upper lip than is used with the horn, e.g., about three-quarters upper, one-quarter lower. But the exact position will depend on the length of the upper lip and the position of the nose.

[*N.B.*—An ingenious means of estimating lip proportions (quoted by Farkas 1962) is by the use of a special mouthpiece rim, on a handle, placed on the lips as though the embouchure is set for playing. The lip adaptation is examined in a mirror attached to a bandsman's music lyre clamped to the instrument. A comparison is made with the mouthpiece of the instrument as set for playing.]

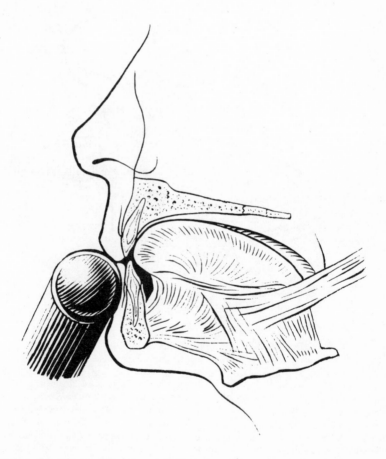

Fig. 6—To show the adaptation of the lips to the flute, where the jaws, face, mouth, teeth, etc., might be considered "within the bounds of the normal".

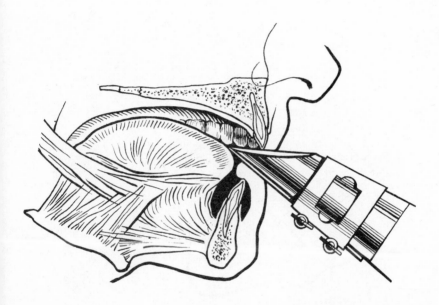

Fig. 7—To show the adaptation of the lips, teeth and tongue to the mouthpiece of the clarinet, where conditions might be considered "within the bounds of the normal".

NOTE: (1) Compression* of lower lip on to the lower incisor teeth by the mouthpiece. (2) Pressure* of upper incisor teeth on to the sloping upper side of mouthpiece. (This would be an average "single-lip" embouchure. In a "double-lip" embouchure the upper lip would be curled under the upper incisor teeth and between them and the sloping upper side of the mouthpiece. The length of the upper lip and relative position of upper front teeth would determine which embouchure would be most suitable.)

*The pressure in both cases is unintentional, but becomes inevitable as playing proceeds, owing to the predominant strength of the elevator muscles of the lower jaw.

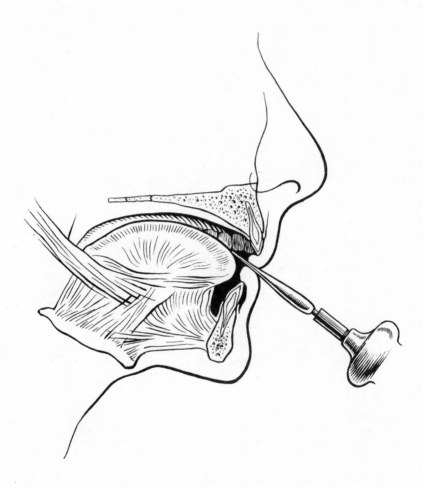

Fig. 8—To show the adaptation of the lips, teeth and tongue to the mouthpiece of the oboe, where the jaws, face, mouth and teeth might be considered "within the bounds of the normal".

NOTE: The "double-lip" embouchure here, as with all double reed instruments, is essential. There is, however, a very specialised difference in detail between the oboe and the bassoon. In this case, note the compression of the lower lip and upper lip against the lower and upper incisor teeth respectively. The bassoon mouthpiece, being much larger, requires more lip and mouth room and a different head of pressure on the air column.

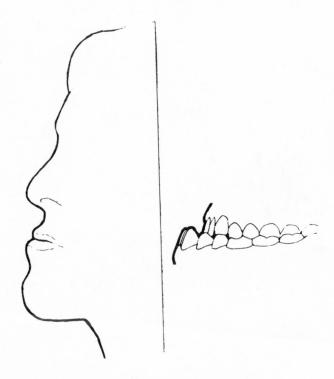

Fig. 9—To show type of face with protruding lower jaw.

NOTE: (1) Protruding chin and sunken upper jaw. (2) Protruding lower front teeth when back teeth are in the individual's normal clenched position.

[*N.B.*—In adapting the embouchure to a brass instrument (compare with Figs. 4 and 5) the instrument needs to be directed more upwards, or the player's head more downwards or a combination of both. Similarly, with a single or double reed instrument, the instrument is directed more upwards in relation to the body of the player (compare with Figs. 7 and 8). Adaptation of the embouchure in flute playing necessitates turning the head of the instrument more outwards and holding it higher on the lower lip so as to enable the air leaving the mouth to be directed across the hole. Alternatively, a similar effect could be produced by the flautist bowing his head to the instrument instead of turning the instrument more outwards.]

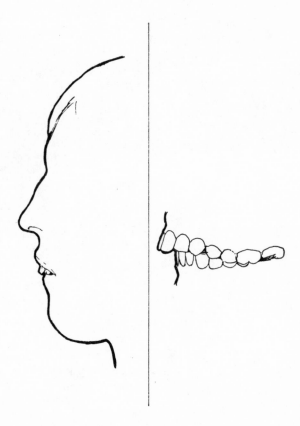

Fig. 10—To show type of face with retruding lower jaw and protruding upper teeth.

NOTE: (1) Upper jaw is prominent and apparently protruding. (2) Prominent and protruding upper front teeth, when back teeth are in the individual's normal clenched position. (3) In adapting the embouchure to a brass or reed instrument in cases of this type, the instrument would need to be directed more downwards or the head of the player more upwards. With the flute the head of the instrument would need to be turned more inwards.

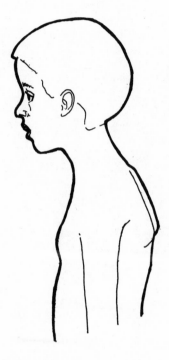

Fig. 11—To show typical appearance of child where continual mouth breathing has occurred due to nasal obstruction "adenoids", comforters, etc.

NOTE: (1) Mouth slightly open. (2) Short, poorly functional upper lip, chin retruded. (3) Sunken chest and rounded shoulders, and head apparently thrust forward.

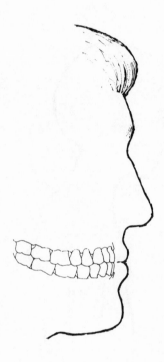

Fig. 12—To show type of face with jaws "within the bounds of the normal".

NOTE: (1) Jaws are "normally" related to one another and teeth are in "normal" (centric) "occlusion" when the back teeth are clenched. (2) When there is no irregularity between individual teeth the appearance is as above.

CHAPTER II

EMBOUCHURE COMFORT AND DISCOMFORT

An embouchure of comfort implies a state of the musician's lips and mouth free from any pain or other distracting influence which enables him to produce the quality of tone he desires, to articulate the sounds he needs and to phrase the music as required. All these activities he is able to carry out spontaneously and with a feeling of ease while his embouchure is in such a state.

A performer with an uncomfortable embouchure, however, seldom plays at what he feels is his best.[11] In an experienced player discomfort can occasionally occur as a result of such annoying things as ulcers of the lips or mouth, a skin rash or boil, or a loose or painful tooth. Under these conditions he is compelled to try to find an alternative position for his mouthpiece, slightly away from the painful area, which will give him an embouchure of maximum, or at least reasonable, comfort. When the troublesome condition returns to normal his habitual embouchure of comfort is again easily assumed and his maximum efficiency is again possible.

The instinct of all experienced players is to select and adopt an embouchure which will permit greatest playing comfort. There are some experienced players, however, whose embouchures have never been entirely comfortable. This is often reflected in their appearance of awkward embouchure adaptation and sometimes in the sounds they produce. A study of their jaws and teeth would probably reveal the cause.

With many beginners and even some advanced players an embouchure of real comfort could be out of their reach, for a reason they might never have considered. It is simply that they have chosen an instrument which demands an adaptation of embouchure to which their lips, jaws and teeth are not entirely suited. It is possible that had the instrument been chosen in the first instance with due regard to these factors and had they heeded the teacher's advice as to suitability, an embouchure of much better comfort might have been achieved, albeit on a different instrument, and much greater and more rapid progress might have been made.

The degree of comfort a player can achieve depends on the mouthpiece of the instrument, the way in which the natural relationship between his upper and lower jaws will allow it to be adapted to his lips, and how far the shape and position of his front teeth might interfere with it. In view of the very detailed variations that exist in the mouthpieces of a single instrument (e.g., variations in the mouthpieces of the clarinet as distinct from those in the mouthpieces of another instrument), and the still greater variations that exist in mouth, jaw and teeth irregularities, the complex subject of embouchure comfort can be only briefly discussed here.

BRASS INSTRUMENT PLAYING

With brass instrument playing small irregularities of the teeth in a vertical direction (such as an elongated tooth) do not seem to matter much. But *projection* of, say, a single tooth in a forward direction can interfere a great deal with blowing. In this case the rim of the cup of the mouthpiece compresses the lip against the offending tooth. An embouchure of comfort may be found by placing the mouthpiece to avoid this area of the lip, provided similar irregularities in the other front teeth do not cause a like embarrassment of the embouchure. The use of a different size of mouthpiece might solve the problem. It can be another mouthpiece of the same instrument or a mouthpiece of another brass instrument, e.g., a change can be made from, say, cornet to trombone. Where the same instrument is to be retained and a change of size of mouthpiece does not materially reduce the discomfort, a dentist might help considerably—for example, by smoothing an offending corner of a tooth or by making a crown on the adjacent tooth to bring it in line and so obliterating the painful protrusion of the offending tooth. This procedure could be carried out, for instance, after testing the effects of a temporary crown. If successful, the whole procedure could be well worth the expense and time involved.

In the teaching of brass instrument playing, distinction was made in the past between the so-called "pressure" and "nonpressure" systems. In the first system the higher notes were obtained by tighter compression of the mouthpiece against the lips. The second system was supposed to produce the higher notes by pressing the lips together tighter, relying only on the decreased size of aperture between the lips, without pressing the mouthpiece tighter against the lips. Time-honoured and ingenious methods were used to demonstrate the "non-pressure" system, for example, by suspending a cornet from the ceiling with a horizontal line on a table or the floor marking the resting position of the suspended instrument. The player was then required to blow certain notes without moving the instrument beyond the line and without touching the instrument with his hands. Since with some practice this was achieved, it gave rise to a remarkably widespread and erroneous belief, especially among bandsmen, that no pressure at all was being used by the mouthpiece against the lips. The gravitational force of the instrument towards the floor was, of course, absorbing the main part of the pressure of the lips against the mouthpiece.

While the intentions of such teaching and the results were no doubt sufficient to impress upon the student the necessity for avoiding excessive pressure of the mouthpiece against the lips, it is surprising how many mature players, bandsmen, as well as students, imagine that no pressure at all is used during their playing other than pressing the lips together. This is quite contrary to the facts. A certain degree of pressure of the mouthpiece against the lips is always necessary. Obviously, the lighter this is, the better. This teaching experiment, nevertheless, had some advantage in so far as it restricted the student to using the *minimum* lip pressure necessary against the mouthpiece for those notes played.

Radiographs taken of some of the foremost exponents of the so-called "non-pressure"[12] system will readily show the difference in pressure of the mouthpiece against the lips between low notes and high notes (see Figs. 13 and 14). The fact is that while these players without doubt use considerably less pressure than many others, pressure, however light, is always used (see Fig. 15). For the sake of accuracy, therefore, it would be far better to speak of a "minimum pressure" system or "light pressure" system rather than of a "non-pressure" system.

When there is continually excessive pressure of the mouthpiece against the lips it will, sooner or later, interfere with an embouchure of comfort. When carried to an extreme it can be

25

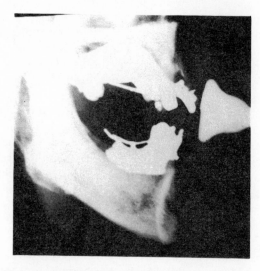

Fig. 13—Radiograph of cornet player. Showing embouchure whilst playing highest note with so-called "non-pressure" system.

NOTE: (1) Distance of mouthpiece from upper incisor teeth. (2) Degree of separation between upper and lower front teeth. (3) Position of hyoid bone, tucked under mandible (lower jaw). Artificial plastic teeth are radiolucent and are not shown.

positively harmful. The author has referred to a case on record of the upper lip being perforated in a trumpet player.[13] Some slighter disfiguration of the upper lip is quite a common occurrence in some experienced players (see Fig. 16). More often than not this is due to a projecting edge or corner of a tooth against which the lip is being pressed by the mouthpiece. Prolonged playing sessions, even without such obstructions, can cause deterioration in embouchure comfort. This is usually due to lack of sufficient rest periods during playing[14] and has often been attributed to the indifference of the composer, arranger or conductor.

Compression of any soft tissues such as skin, mucous membrane, muscle (such as in the lips) tends to restrict the blood supply, at first causing blanching of the skin, then numbness, and, if excessive and prolonged, even damage. Blood carries oxygen to the tissues and carries away waste products. Both of these

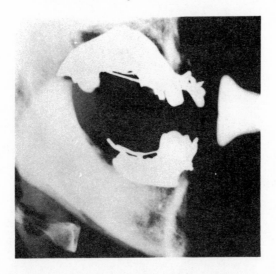

Fig. 14—Radiograph of same player as in Fig. 13. Showing embouchure whilst
playing lowest note.

NOTE: (1) Increased separation of mouthpiece from upper incisors. (2) Increased
separation between upper and lower incisors. (3) Depression of hyoid bone, now
clearly seen, in order to increase intra-oral volume for much lower note. Artificial
plastic teeth are radiolucent and are not shown.

functions, the first by the arterial blood and the second by the
venous blood, cannot be impeded for too long without harmful
effect. For this and other reasons, such as breathing, wind
musicians need more frequent and longer rest periods during
playing than either string or percussion musicians. If the wind
musician is to play at his best, it is essential that these requirements should be recognised so that he is given the opportunity
of maintaining an embouchure of maximum comfort with its
obvious advantages.

SINGLE REED INSTRUMENTS

Where the condition of the teeth and jaws is "normal" in a
young adult there is an uninterrupted curve in the region of the
cutting edges of the upper and lower front teeth. With some
individuals these teeth are already thin from before backwards

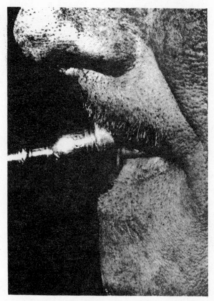

Fig. 15—The near-perfect embouchure on a cornet using "minimum pressure" system.
Demonstrated in one of the finest British soloists.

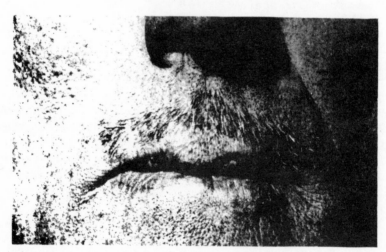

Fig. 16—Showing same player as in Fig. 15.
NOTE: One slightly rotated and slightly protruding upper front tooth has caused a slight change in the shape of the lips over many years.

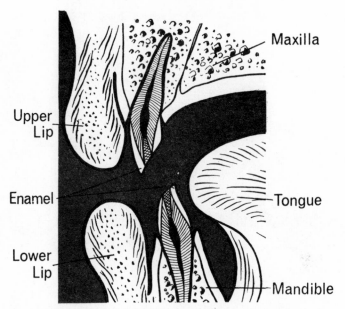

Fig. 17—Section (sagittal) through the jaws and teeth.

NOTE: Chisel-shaped incisor teeth with sharp enamel edge towards lip in upper and towards tongue in lower.

[*N.B.*—This is the appearance in a mouth with normal jaws, teeth and occlusion ("bite"), in an adult of about 30 years or more. It is due to wearing down of enamel and unequal attrition of dentine and enamel. Dentine is softer.]

and sharp, somewhat knife-like. With the lapse of time and continual attrition and unequal wear of the two different hard tissues (enamel and dentine) of which the crowns of the teeth are constructed, they take on a very chisel-like form having a sharp edge towards the lip in the upper jaw and towards the tongue in the lower (see Fig. 17). When one or both lips are curled over these teeth backwards into the mouth there is a tendency for a linear cut to form inside the lip or lips.

This is particularly noticeable with the *single reed* instrumentalists (see Fig. 18). Where a "single lip embouchure" is used, that is, where the line of the cutting edges of the lower front teeth is covered by the lower lip (on which the reed rests)

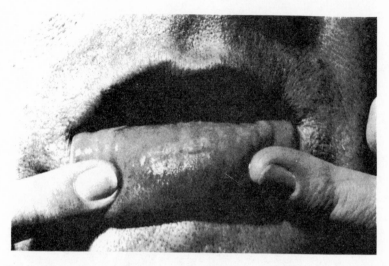

Fig. 18—Linear impression in lower lip, due to cutting effect of lower incisor teeth, in very experienced clarinet soloist. Dentition is normal and teeth regularly positioned as in Fig. 17.

[*N.B.*—The effect is far greater in some players where the teeth and jaws are not so regular.]

the top front teeth close on the mouthpiece and discomfort is caused by this cutting tendency. Where the line of the cutting edges is irregular and tortuous in a horizontal direction, due to individual teeth being rotated, and the lower lip is curled over these teeth, discomfort or pain can be more acute at certain points on the inside of the lip.

The line of the cutting edges might be irregular in a vertical direction due to the incisal edge of one or more teeth being at a higher level than the adjacent ones. Similar discomfort is common in these cases. Then again both irregularities might be present at the same time (see Fig. 19). There might also be small spaces between adjacent teeth or large spaces due to absence of a tooth or teeth (see Fig. 20). In such conditions the player can find his lip being pressed into the space, often with a good deal of discomfort or pain.

Where a "double lip embouchure" is used, the upper lip is curled downwards over the upper front teeth, acting as a buffer

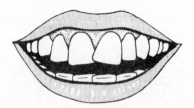

Fig. 19—To show irregularity of upper front teeth.

NOTE: (1) Overlapping, tilting and different vertical level of front teeth. (2) This would cause sharp corners to dig into upper lip curled over these teeth, e.g., in reed instrument playing. (3) Brass mouthpiece would press lip against protruding corners. Alternately, a similar condition could occur in the lower teeth.

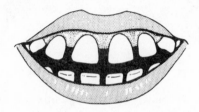

Fig. 20—To show natural spaces between upper front teeth.

NOTE: These teeth could cause "biting" into the upper lip curled over them in reed instrument playing. The upper lip could sometimes become trapped in a space during a long playing session.

[*N.B.*—To prevent this, see Chapter on "Embouchure Aids".]

between them and the mouthpiece. In addition the lower lip is curled inwards as above. Consequently, discomfort may occur in the upper lip, as well as in the lower lip. Frequently in an otherwise almost perfect dentition, there exists a natural space in the mid-line between the upper front teeth (see Fig. 21). Such a condition is common in individuals with broad faces. Where the upper lip is also long and is conveniently used to cover the upper front teeth the lip is sometimes caught up into the space between the two central incisors. This can become extremely painful during a lengthy session of playing.

DOUBLE REED INSTRUMENTS

In the case of the *double reed* instrumentalists the irregularities mentioned above can cause similar problems regarding em-

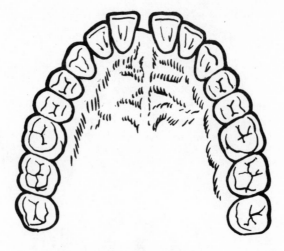

Fig. 21—Natural space in mid-line between upper front teeth in an otherwise normal upper jaw.

NOTE: Free corners which can dig into upper lip curled over these teeth and space into which lip can be pressed.

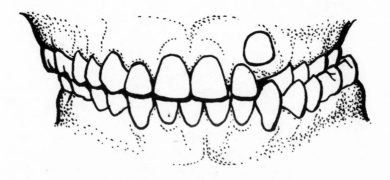

Fig. 22—Outstanding canine tooth occurring on upper left side.

NOTE: (1) Canine tooth high up on left side and tilted. (2) Upper lip in "pursed" smiling position, as in flute playing, stretched over these teeth can be painful on the left side. Any other wind instrument could also be painful to an upper lip with this condition. (3) Lower jaw is "normal" on subject's right side, i.e., top back teeth overlapping lower. On left side top back teeth are clenched inside the lower, giving a swollen effect to lower jaw on left side (compare with Fig. 25).

bouchure comfort, although varying with the different types of double reed used, e.g., oboe, bassoon.

FLUTE

With the *Flute*, lip trouble of the kind mentioned is less common, unless irregularities in the lower front teeth are more pronounced. Consequently the discomfort, if any, is usually in the lower lip. In the upper jaw an outstanding canine tooth (which is by no means rare) can be a cause for much discomfort in flute playing by interfering with the control of the upper lip (see Fig. 22).

Before proceeding to the next chapter a few words about dentures might be appropriate. Artificial teeth, unless specially constructed to embouchure requirements of the kind peculiar to the individual player, can be a problem to embouchure comfort during playing. While not always so, it is frequently the case. A dental surgeon's aim is to construct a denture for the purposes of eating and speaking in comfort and restoring appearance. This task is difficult in itself and in some cases the difficulties are almost insuperable, to the completely blissful ignorance of the patient. It is unfortunately true that in many cases of wind musicians the strains and stresses used in eating run quite counter to those necessary for embouchure comfort in playing certain instruments. Often the problem can be solved by the player having, of necessity, two sets made, the one to conform to eating and the other to give maximum embouchure comfort during playing.[15]

In some individuals loss of certain teeth can be a hazard to their playing,[16] and for this reason particular attention is directed to the chapter on "Care of the Embouchure."

CHAPTER III

EMBOUCHURE POTENTIAL

The "Embouchure Potential" of a given player, or beginner, on a certain instrument, is a term I am introducing to indicate the estimated maximum extent to which his embouchure can develop, within a given time, to produce a high degree of quality of tone without undue effort. It should be emphasized that the student's professor or teacher is probably the best judge of this. No book can replace the expert teacher of an instrument, even though it might help to clarify the problems of embouchure and indicate possible cures as part of this work tries to do; and it may also assist the teacher in arriving at a more accurate assessment of the student's embouchure potential.

So far as embouchure is concerned, the way in which a student or beginner can develop will depend on a number of factors. The most prominent of these are the relationship of his jaws to each other; the position, form and arrangement of his front teeth; the form, texture and manœuvrability of his lips; and the instrument to which he hopes to adapt all these factors. Since different instruments demand different adaptations of embouchure, there are certain faces where the muscular arrangement obstructs the conformity of the lips to the embouchure demands of the instrument. Such muscular restriction can be responsible for hindering progress on the instrument or, when playing has reached a certain standard, halting any further improvement. Human nature, however, being what it is, many an undaunted student often plods along, blissfully unaware both of his initial disadvantage and of the fact that he will probably reach only a certain degree of mediocrity after many years of devoted effort. In these circumstances it is likely that a less hardy and not so persistent spirit will even fall by the way. On the other hand, some players in spite of such handicaps do, in fact, reach a very high standard as wind musicians. This, however, is due to a number of compensating factors, not the least of which is sheer determination by the musician.

When all is considered, it is the teacher's advice that is of greatest importance as regards the pupil's embouchure potential, but the full responsibility for failure cannot be his if the pupil persists in his own choice of instrument, particularly if it is against the advice given by the teacher. If, after an initial number of probationary lessons, and diligent practice by the pupil, certain embouchure troubles persist, or certain embouchure faults are repeated habitually, a re-appraisal might be made of facial type.

In jaw relationship, as mentioned earlier (Chapter I), three distinct classes are in evidence (see Figs. 9, 10 and 12), although there are innumerable variations of all three. These three main classes are in an antero-posterior (forward to backward) direction. In addition to these three classes there are some other rather less frequent variations in jaw relationship, where deviations of the lower jaw might be to one side or the other. These and other variations are included collectively under Class IV below.

There are, therefore, four classes to be discussed, but before doing so, there is a matter of much importance which should be considered briefly, particularly by teachers of brass instrument playing. It is the limitation of movements of the lower jaw and special attention is drawn to the embouchures of brass players in Class III below. When any variation is to be made in the opening of the mouth *it is the lower jaw alone which moves.* The lower jaw is permitted certain degrees of movement by a somewhat complicated hinge and ball and socket joint. The actual movements are carried out by a complex of muscles. For simplicity this joint is shown without its supporting fibrous capsule, ligaments and muscles in Fig. 23. The lower jaw bone (mandible) does not articulate with the upper jaw bone (maxilla) but with the temporal bone which forms part of the side of the head and face and part of the base of the skull. Hence the joint is known as the *temporo-mandibular joint.*

When the mouth is closed and the teeth of both jaws oppose each other, as in the clenched position, they are said to be in occlusion. This differs from an articulation, which is a joint. The temporo-mandibular joint is separated into two compartments, an upper and a lower, each containing what is known as synovial fluid (acting as a sort of lubricant). Between the two compartments is an articular disc of cartilage (see Fig. 24a). The head

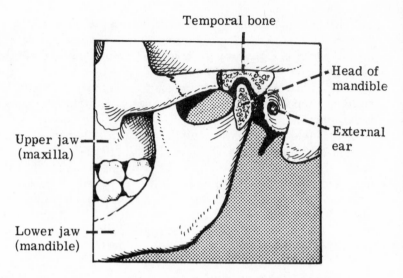

Fig. 23—Temporo-mandibular joint.

NOTE: (1) Head of lower jaw (mandible) articulates with temporal bone. (2) Teeth of lower jaw are in occlusion with those of upper jaw, i.e., are in clenched position. (3) Head of mandible cannot move backwards beyond this position. It is prevented by the bony socket of the temporal bone and by the bony part of the external ear, as well as the cusps of the upper teeth.

of the lower jaw (also known as the condylar process, or condyle) may be felt as it moves in front of the ear, on opening or closing the mouth.

The lower compartment contains the condyle and allows a hinge type of movement as in opening and closing the mouth. The upper compartment allows for a gliding movement. Forward gliding movement occurs in addition to the hinge movement in opening the mouth. A forward gliding movement of the head of the mandible also occurs in thrusting the lower jaw forward. In bringing the jaw back, the head of the mandible glides back again, but only to its original position in the socket in normal circumstances. Having returned to the position of rest, which is with the back teeth clenched, it *cannot be brought back farther* except to a negligible degree. Any further backward movement of the head of the mandible is prevented by the back of the

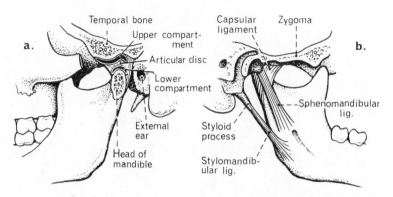

Fig. 24—Temporo-mandibular joint. Showing section (sagittal) through the joint and capsular ligament.

a.—*Outside appearance (facial side).*

NOTE: (1) Molar teeth in clenched position. (2) Upper and lower compartment of joint separated by cartilaginous articular disc surrounded by strong fibrous capsular ligament. Pain would occur on lower jaw being forced backwards against bony external ear. Stylomandibular ligament is excluded here.

b.—*Inside appearance (within mouth).*

NOTE: (1) Head of mandible in socket of temporal bone, which would prevent any appreciable backward movement of mandible. (2) Upper molar teeth excluded.

socket of the temporal bone, the strong capsule embracing the joint, the strong ligaments supporting the joint from the inside (see **Fig.** 24b) and the various muscles attached to the bones involved.

In certain individuals, where the capsular ligament is weak, excessive opening of the mouth causes the head of the mandible to come right forward and "jump" the eminence of the temporal bone, which would normally prevent such movement. This sometimes results in dislocation of the joint and temporarily fixes it in this open position. Such a condition is easily corrected by the doctor or dentist. In the very young and elderly, the head of the mandible is more flattened so that some limited backward movement, beyond the clenched position of the lower jaw, is permitted by the joint.

It should be emphasized that the classification below is for wind musicians only and is not to be confused with that used by dentists in orthodontia, of which it is a modification.

Class I.

This is the normal relationship between the jaws and is shown in Fig. 12. The embouchure potential here is admirable for almost any wind instrument, with, however, one provision. The biting edges should be even in a vertical or horizontal direction in the front teeth. It will be noted that in this class the arch of the upper teeth slightly overlaps the arch of the lower teeth all the way round. It will also be noted that the tip of each upper back tooth bites a little behind its fellow in the lower jaw to the extent of approximately one-quarter to one-third of a tooth, allowing each lower tooth to be in contact with two upper teeth; i.e., they interdigitate. This is known as normal occlusion. The temporo-mandibular joint will not allow the lower jaw to move behind this position but it will allow forward and side-to-side movement as well as hinge movement as in opening the mouth.

Should there be no appreciable protrusion of any corners of the upper front teeth, and no protrusion of a single front tooth, the embouchure potential would be favourable for any brass instrument. Protrusion of either would tend to disturb an embouchure of comfort, depending on the extent of protrusion and the sensitivity of the lips.

Elongation of a front tooth above the horizontal line of the other front teeth in the lower jaw would hamper the single reed instrumentalist by irritating his lower lip. A similar irregularity in the upper front teeth would disturb the "double lip embouchure", used always in double reed instruments and often with the clarinet, by irritating also the upper lip.

Class II.

Where there is a receding lower jaw rendering the upper front teeth prominent when the back teeth are clenched (see Fig. 10), or where the upper front teeth are prominent without necessarily involving a receding lower jaw, the embouchure is limited in scope. The scope of adaptability depends on the length of the upper lip and its manœuvrability as well as its sensitivity (some individuals can bear discomfort or pain in the lip more than others, so that stamina in practice and performance is potentially greater). "Double-lip" embouchures on double or single reed instruments can be a handicap where the upper lip is short, depending on the individual's nervous condition. For example, the very "nervous" type would probably "take" more pain on his upper lip than he could reasonably endure, because it is tightly stretched over his upper teeth. The "lymphatic" type on the other hand (who never seems to worry so much about pain because, in fact, he does not really *feel* it so much) copes with much more ease. The "lymphatic" type, however, probably has less of the "artistic" potential.

The player of the single reed instrument usually rests his front upper teeth on the sloping top 'of the mouthpiece, e.g., the clarinet.

The.points worthy of note here, in the consideration of the embouchure potential of these players by the professor or teacher are:

(1) The structural condition of the upper front teeth, particularly the enamel, should, as far as possible, be good and strong. Large carious cavities between the teeth can sooner or later be the cause for the corners of the teeth to chip away or collapse, and possibly result in loss of a tooth or teeth.

(2) The condition of the gums should be healthy. If it is not, there is a chance that, in this form of embouchure (which is by far the most common), the upper front teeth may become loose.

(3) Consideration should be given to the wearing of dentures. In any of these cases regular dental care is obviously of great importance to the player.

In this class most instruments need to be held down and nearer the body (see Fig. 10). With players of brass instruments a reasonably slight protrusion of the upper front teeth does not influence the embouchure potential much, provided they are well aligned and present an uninterrupted outward curve. Excessive outward protrusion could do so if the upper lip is short. The lip would require undue stretching to separate and buffer these teeth from the cup of the mouthpiece and this stretching in a long session of playing tends to tire the lip more rapidly. It can as a result influence the rate of progress. Where the alignment of the upper front teeth is interrupted by, for example, the rotation of a single tooth, a corner of this tooth can be a positive nuisance, making the player constantly aware of the pressure against the upper lip by the cup of the mouthpiece. If left untreated this condition could also greatly influence embouchure potential.

As with the reed instrument, the brass player with this class of embouchure tends to hold the instrument more downwards, nearer the body, and the flute player turns the head of the instrument more inwards or tilts his head more backwards.

In flute playing these conditions do not create the same effect. It is far less, unless the alignment of the upper front teeth is very bad, e.g., as a result of overlapping or rotated front teeth or of outstanding canine teeth. These irregular teeth could interfere with the stretching and manœuvrability of the upper lip.

Class III.

Where there is a protrusion of the lower jaw or where the upper jaw is underdeveloped, giving a similar appearance when the back teeth are clenched (see Fig. 9), the embouchure is again limited in scope for wind instrument playing.

"Double-lip" embouchure in reed instrument playing here might be more easily accomplished than in Class II cases, but more difficulty could be encountered in adapting the lower front teeth. In Class III most instruments need to be held upwards and further away from the body than in the other classes, in order to adapt upper and lower lips to the mouthpiece of the instrument. For practical purposes the lower jaw can be moved only forwards from the clenched position; the distance the jaw can be moved voluntarily behind the clenched position is negligible. Since the jaw is already jutting forwards in its natural position, the possible embouchure adaptation is limited.

A good example of this limitation is in the playing of brass instruments. Teachers of these instruments sometimes insist on advising the pupil to adapt his embouchure in such a way that the upper and lower front teeth should be brought into a vertical straight line, i.e., that the lower teeth should not be brought in front of the upper ones and vice versa. Reference to page 36, describing the limitation of movement of the temporo-mandibular joint, will demonstrate that such advice in these Class III cases is futile. It is just not possible for these players to bring the lower front teeth back into vertical alignment with the upper ones. The only way this can ·be done is by artificial means (i.e., either by an embouchure aid used while playing, or by artificial bridge-work or a denture specially constructed by the dental surgeon to bring the upper lip forward to allow alignment with the lower lip). In some selected cases of this kind artificial rehabilitation of the mouth might be planned artistically by means of the bridge-work mentioned, so that the mouth can now be easily adapted to both the embouchure required and the normal functions of eating, and so on. But in other more complicated cases such rehabilitation might not be possible or advisable, and here it might be better for the dental surgeon to design a denture-like appliance to be worn only during playing. There being no two cases alike, each has to be treated on its own merits. In flute-playing, the head of the instrument resting on or under the lower lip would need to be turned more outwards to assist the direction of the air flow across the hole without straining the upper lip.

Class IV.

The appearances of Classes II and III above are usually due to an interference of one kind or another with the natural development of the jaws since childhood. Such an interference usually affects either jaw as a whole. There are other cases where development in childhood is different on each side of the face, so that, say, the lower jaw is larger on one side than the other. Looking at the face from the front it would appear that the lower jaw is swollen on one side (see Fig. 25). Inside the mouth, however, with the back teeth clenched, while the teeth might meet normally on the unaffected side (that is, with the upper teeth slightly outside the lower teeth), on the affected, ("swollen" side), the lower side teeth jut out away from the upper teeth (see Fig. 26).

Another less common example likely to be problematic for the teacher and his pupil is a case where, when the back teeth are in the natural clenched position, the upper and lower front teeth are a good way from meeting so that there is a gap—quite wide in some individuals. This is known as "open-bite". In such a case it is quite impossible to bring the front teeth of the lower jaw in contact with the front teeth of the upper jaw (see Fig. 27). A case of this kind might have a reasonable embouchure potential for the larger intra-oral mouthpiece, such as saxophone or clarinet, but it might have a poor potential for some brass instruments except those with larger mouthpieces. All these unusual cases, and many others, might therefore, be collectively dealt with together under Class IV.

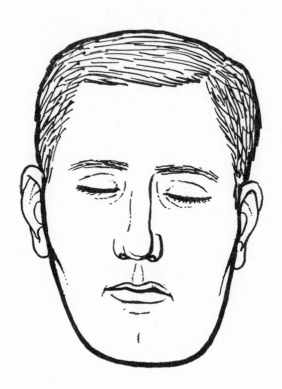

Fig. 25—Unequal development between the two sides of lower jaw.

NOTE: (1) Swollen effect on subject's left side of lower jaw. (2) "Flattened" effect on right side when compared with left side.

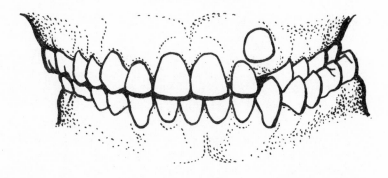

Fig. 26—Unequal development of jaws. Appearance inside mouth of condition in Fig. 25.

NOTE: (1) Lower teeth bite outside upper teeth on subject's left side. (2) On other side "bite" is normal, i.e., upper teeth overlap lower ones.

[*N.B.*—Such a "bite" or occlusion is not necessarily due to unequal development of the jaws themselves. It can be the result of an abnormal development in the *relationship* of the lower to the upper jaw. Such abnormalities can be the result, for example, of the premature loss of "milk" teeth. This could cause permanent teeth to erupt in eccentric positions. There are numerous other causes, such as eccentric facial habits during bone growth in childhood.]

(*The presence of the outstanding canine tooth is discussed in the chapter on embouchure comfort.*)

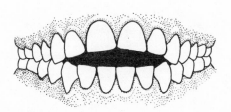

Fig. 27—"Open-bite".

NOTE: (1) Clenched position (occlusion) of back teeth of upper and lower jaws. (2) Separation between upper and lower incisor teeth. This is sometimes thought to be an advantage in playing the larger brass instruments with large mouthpieces, e.g., trombone, tuba, etc.

[*N.B.*—"Open-bite" can be due to thumb-sucking, or to premature loss of back "milk" teeth which allows permanent teeth to erupt comparatively early in molar regions, or to prolonged use of "comforters" in childhood.]

A few selected examples will now be considered for the benefit of teachers and others interested:

(1) There are a reasonable number of individuals who have broad faces and correspondingly broad jaws, yet with teeth not broad enough to fill the wide sweep of the gums. As a result, there is a large gap between the upper two front teeth and perhaps smaller spaces on each side (see Fig. 28). The effect of such an arrangement of the teeth in playing a reed instrument, particularly one where a double-lip embouchure is used, is to allow unhindered and undesired penetration of the isolated teeth into the tender mucous membrane and the muscle of the lip. It has been known, even in foremost artists, for the lip under such conditions to be trapped in the space between the teeth and rendered raw and even mutilated after prolonged playing. One celebrated player even had to drag the trapped lip from between the teeth following a magnificent and unforgettable performance.

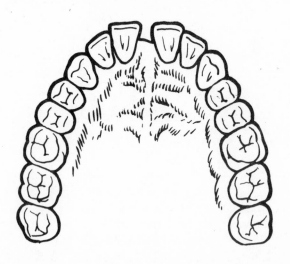

Fig. 28—Space between upper central incisors.

[*N.B.*—This is common in individuals with broad faces. Such a condition would be troublesome with the double-lip embouchure of reed instrument players.]

(2) Severe overcrowding or overlapping of the teeth sometimes occurs, due to inadequate development of the jaws in childhood or to arrested development or collapse of the jaws following premature loss of the deciduous ("milk") teeth. This last condition can often result in the permanent teeth erupting in various undesirable positions (see Fig. 29); or sometimes even in their not erupting into the mouth at all. Some of these badly positioned teeth might annoy or penetrate even a resting slack lip and interfere with normal functions, such as eating. In an embouchure adaptation with lips stretched over, or pressed against, such teeth wind instrument playing can be a painful or trying business.

Fig. 29—To illustrate overcrowding of the teeth with abnormal occlusion.

NOTE: (1) Irregularity of position of the teeth in both jaws. (2) Upper teeth bite inside lower ones on subject's left side. (3) "Squashed" appearance of "bite".
[*N.B.*—Probably unfavourable for intra-oral wind instruments; probably unfavourable also for brass instrument with small mouthpiece. In some selected cases it is possible for the dental surgeon to rehabilitate such a mouth by artificial means, e.g., bridge-work, etc. (see Chapter on "Embouchure Aids").]

(3) In a number of cases which are, however, usually rare, there are present in the jaws supernumerary teeth, that is, teeth above the normal number (see Fig. 30). These are due to developmental abnormalities. The teeth can be duplicated, in some rare cases in great number. Where such cases go uncorrected or untreated, embouchure problems can be great. Often such supernumerary teeth are pointed or conical and on lip pressure in embouchure adaptation can give considerable pain to the lips.

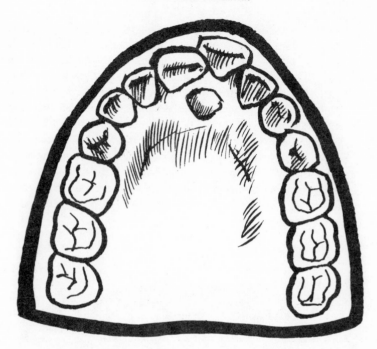

Fig. 30—Supernumerary tooth in front of hard palate.

NOTE: Displacement forwards of left upper central incisor in otherwise normal 'arch". First premolar is missing and space closed on each side due to early extractions—presumably to make room for overcrowding.

[*N.B.*—Early dental attention might have prevented the "displacement". The presence of such a tooth could be troublesome to any wind instrumentalist.]

(4) There may be congenital conditions where teeth are absent in the jaws and will never, therefore, erupt into the mouth. This may or may not give rise to embouchure problems, depending on the alignment of the remaining teeth.

(5) Gaps in the side of the jaws due to missing teeth following extractions which are not replaced artificially might allow the cheek or buccinator muscle (see Figs. 1 and 2) to puff out in an uncontrollable manner and puzzle or annoy the professor or teacher. This is due to the missing "girders" (side teeth) so necessary for the support of the embouchure musculature.

(6) A not uncommon irregularity of the teeth, which presents a problem in embouchure potential, is the outstanding canine tooth (see Figs. 22 and 26). In this case the canine tooth (usually the upper, although sometimes the lower) being late in erupting, has emerged with its point jutting outwards high into the side of the upper lip. When this occurs, it often does so on both sides. Should there be a short upper lip this can be a great disadvantage on any instrument, but particularly on the double reed instruments. The lip, in stretching over the front teeth, can be very painful and the mucous membrane on the inside even pierced. With a longer upper lip there is comparatively less pain, but a degree of embouchure discomfort can remain. In dealing with this problem, each case must be considered solely on its merits, the answer seldom being simply extraction of the offending tooth, since sometimes a considerable amount of contraction of the hard and soft tissues (i.e., bone and gum) takes place in the upper jaw over a varying period of time. This can give rise to other embouchure complications later. A dental surgeon or orthodontist should be consulted. In the young (pre-adolescent), the problem of the outstanding canine tooth can often be corrected by expert treatment, and the advice of the dental surgeon or orthodontist should be sought. Such treatment and advice could be invaluable to the would-be musician.

The above cases are everyday examples of the innumerable variations that might exist in students or pupils confronting a teacher of a wind instrument. It will, therefore, be appreciated why it is best to place these collectively under Class IV of Embouchure Potential. Any of them might present a perplexing problem in advising the choice of a suitable wind instrument. It should be remembered, however, that many of these mouths can be treated and made much more adaptable by such means as embouchure aids, or by "rehabilitation" of the mouth with bridge-work and other elaborate dental appliances.

From all that has been discussed in this chapter it becomes more apparent what value can be placed on a full dental report together with models of the teeth and jaws. The assessment can

47

best be made by comparing the individual's case with the "normal". The above classification, given solely for the purpose of wind instrument teachers and their pupils, is a much simplified modification of one used commonly in dental surgery in its highly specialised branch known as Orthodontia.

It will no doubt be clear from the above that embouchure potential is a matter worthy of much consideration by all concerned in wind instrument playing and not only by the player himself. Where the latter is an amateur and is playing or learning to play for sheer delight or amusement he could be encouraged with enthusiasm and would no doubt benefit by being guided, if he so agrees, to the instrument which permits his maximum scope in playing. But where the student intends to follow a career in playing a wind instrument much more serious matters are involved. He or his parents might be investing a considerable amount of money and time in the attempt to have him trained to become at least a reasonably good professional musician. In doing this they would expect him to reap a due reward. Even more important is the consideration, in the U.K. at any rate, of the investment of public or private funds in a candidate for a scholarship or other award.

It is in everyone's interest that the student intending to become a professional musician be given the opportunity of wisest choice of instrument. Where some reasonably correctable embouchure defect occurs, it should be noticed and put right, if possible at the outset, at whatever expense, no matter who is to be responsible for its payment. It would therefore appear obvious that the professor's or teacher's responsibility is not a light one. Where, however, the student intends to study the wind instrument as a means to advance to another branch of music, such as composing, conducting and so on, his initial or later embouchure troubles are not likely to be of such significance.

For further information on Embouchure Comfort and Embouchure Potential the reader is referred to Dental Problems in Wind Instrument Playing *by M. M. Porter, published by the* British Dental Association.

CHAPTER IV

THE EMBOUCHURE AND RESONANCE

All wind instruments require a "generator" whose vibration initiates the sound. This generator (sometimes referred to as the "initiator", "vibrator", "interruptor" or "prime mover") is the reed in the clarinet and saxophone attached to the "tone chamber". It is the double reed in the oboe, bassoon, and so on; it is the edge of the hole against which air is directed as in the flute; or it is the free edges of the portion of the lips within the cup of the mouthpiece as in brass instruments. The generator then excites the column of air within the instrument to vibrate and thereby "resonate". This column of air is referred to as the "resonator". The generator and resonator constitute a coupled dynamic system.[17]

The frequency of the resonating column of air can be controlled by changing its effective length. This can be done by means of opening or closing the holes (either by keys or by fingers or by both) in the woodwind instruments, or by means of the pistons or slide in brass. The air in the cavities of the head, mouth, throat and chest (see Figs. 42, 42A and 46), is also said to be set in vibration.[18] Exactly how this happens is not clear, but that its management by the player has a profound effect on the sound produced (e.g., tone colour) there is no doubt, as may be observed by listening to different players on the very same instrument. The embouchure is largely responsible for controlling the pressure and direction of the air into the mouthpiece. It is in effect a coupling mechanism during playing between the air supply of the player and his instrument.

Before any appreciable sound can be produced by the generator (e.g., the reed or the lips), it must be set into a series of regular vibrations of sufficient strength. The player does this by placing the mouthpiece in an optimum position in relation to the path of the exhaled air and this air must be at a certain degree of pressure. The generator at first offers some resistance to vibration which is then overcome by the sufficiency of air pressure. The generator now vibrates by virtue of its own elasticity and in so doing sets up pressure pulsations in the air column which are taken up by the resonator—i.e., by the air column within the instrument—which now dominates.

Although each instrument, in a general sense, has its own basic sound, each particular player develops his own peculiar sound. The sound quality might be enhanced by the special mouthpiece, reed, or even the whole instrument the player chooses to use. Within certain limits, however, he is able to adapt his embouchure to changed conditions such as a new instrument, but is still able to produce a sound characteristic of himself. Some players have a wide range of adaptability to changed conditions of this kind; with others the range is much narrower. Certain players, for example, prefer the resistance of the generator to be substantially greater than that which other players could possibly tolerate. The latter would perhaps be much disturbed, unless the response of the generator were practically instantaneous.

It is doubtful whether the response can be absolutely instantaneous since an interval of time, however imperceptible to the ear, would elapse before the generator would be set into vibration. The experienced player, aware of this, regulates his embouchure and breathing accordingly. The way in which the player co-ordinates his air supply with the generator and resonator by means of his embouchure and breathing determines the quality of sound he produces. He then also attempts to express and, with his tongue, phrase the music according to his own interpretation.

One has heard eminent teachers of wind instruments refer to the mouth as the resonator. Such a description might be true of the singer, but from purely scientific evidence it would be more accurate to refer to the "vibrating" air within the wind musician's mouth, head, throat and chest cavities as a "supplementary resonator". The resonating column of air within the instrument might be referred to as the "primary resonator". This is probably why teachers, aware of the influence of the "supplementary resonator", so often advise the pupil to "imagine you are singing when playing".

The technique alone of an experienced professional player is often casually expected to be immaculate, in spite of the laborious work required over the years to develop it. There

50

might be some informed listeners who are surprisingly in-different to the efforts of the player, even to the extent of regarding this immaculate technique as nothing more than a "gymnastic" display. The effect on these same listeners, however, might be markedly different when the player is able to produce a fine and highly attractive quality of tone, in addition to such a technique. In the presence of such a tone the occasional lapse in small details of technique might even go unnoticed by all but a few of the audience. The true artist, no doubt, possesses both to an outstanding degree and manages an ease of co-ordination of embouchure, breathing and technique which fascinates his audience and colleagues alike. Often, in fact, he or she becomes an idol, on whose playing many instrumentalists, professional as well as amateur model their own playing.

To reach this high level a wind instrumentalist needs to study, practise and develop to the best of his ability his control of the "primary resonator" within the instrument, and of the "supple-mentary resonator" within himself, as well as his technique. His embouchure and breathing may be deciding factors through which he is able to accomplish this. His own individuality and musicianship do of course dominate and drive, since what he is trying to achieve is a matter of taste and in this there is con-siderable variation among different players; but it is his em-bouchure, breathing and technique which determine the scope of his possible achievement. Some limitations there will always be, such as the player's emotional and physical state, the condition of his hearing apparatus, the atmosphere in which he plays, and so on.

It is an advantage during or after playing to observe the reactions of critical experts to one's own efforts if only to note what displeases them. Tape recordings can help in this respect, when the same supposed tonal or breathing weakness can be played back for self-criticism. One's own playing can usefully be compared to and contrasted with records of the masters. Later, watching a live performance by the artist can be a most instructive experience. If one is close enough, one can note the way he manipulates his lips, face and neck muscles, how and when he replenishes breath. Such observations can give the student a clue to the "supplementary resonance" the soloist adds to the "primary resonance" of the instrument, resulting in the "total resonance" or tone quality he achieves.

"Primary resonance" depends largely on the designing of the instrument itself, its quality of material, the way it is constructed, its mouthpiece, reed, and so forth. The instrument best suited to the player need not necessarily be the most expensive, although it is unlikely that a cheap instrument will give the greatest satisfaction. Consultation with the professor or teacher would in all probability help considerably in this respect.

Resonance is but a small branch of the much wider subject of Acoustics. In wind instrument playing it is still more confined, being associated inseparably with breathing and breath control. It has been regarded in this chapter only in so far as it is related to the embouchure, as the title of the chapter implies. The physics of the subject have been intentionally excluded.

CHAPTER V

THE EMBOUCHURE AND BREATHING

The sound produced in a musical wind instrument is caused by the initial vibration of a body in the path of the column of air blown into it (e.g., the generator, as mentioned in Chapter IV). The vibrating body has been referred to also as the "initiator", the "vibrator", the "prime mover", "excitor", "interruptor", etc. In the clarinet and saxophone it is the single reed against the lay of the mouthpiece and the tone chamber. With the oboe, bassoon and similar instruments it is the double reed. In the case of all the brass instruments it is the parts of the lips immediately surrounding the column of air passing through them, however they might be fashioned to produce the desired tone. The flute sound is produced by the vibration of the material surrounding the hole across which air is blown in spite of the profound influence the lips have upon this. Following all these modes of initiating or generating the sounds on the different instruments, the column of air within the particular instrument is then set in vibration and resonates.

The expired air, provided by the lungs to create the vibration of the generator, requires control of direction of flow as well as control of pressure of flow before the vibrating body can be heard. In addition, it requires control of maintenance of flow and pressure should the music demand it, but any such demands can be fulfilled only within certain limitations and it would, therefore, be a considerable advantage for the composer or arranger as well as the conductor to recognize such limitations.

Breath control is of utmost importance in the playing of any wind instrument for at least two apparent reasons. Firstly, because the instrument could not be played well, or at all, without it. Secondly, because, since breathing is also obviously essential to life, it must be subjected to very strict discipline in order that the essential function of breathing may proceed with the least embarrassment while the expired air is used to the greatest advantage in playing the instrument. In this second respect it would appear that wind instrument playing differs considerably from all other musical instrument playing, however much more difficult in other ways some of the latter may be.

Whatever specialised means might be required in breath control for each instrument, it is an advantage to know something of the anatomy and physiology of the breathing apparatus required for *all* wind instruments. It would be hardly feasible, for instance, to expect a pupil to do something with a part of his anatomy over which he had no control. Nor would it be feasible to expect direct controlled action from a certain organ or muscle when in fact the action is initiated by another organ or muscle,[19] or group of muscles. In this respect it would be eminently desirable for a professor or teacher of a wind instrument to have a *detailed* knowledge of the physiology of breathing in his background of training and experience. He could then choose to apply such methods as he advocates, with the knowledge that he is backed by authoritative scientific evidence.

It is beyond the scope of this work to provide such detailed information, but for interested readers the references at the end of the book list some recent authoritative studies on the subject.

However, an account is given below[20] of some of the essential anatomical and physiological data regarding the breathing apparatus in so far as it concerns the wind musician. Its scope in application to playing depends on the musician's own peculiar physical make-up, the way he uses it and, perhaps most important of all, the way he is taught to use it. The following account is intended to illustrate the salient points of:

(1) The Chest Cavity or Thorax, particularly the intercostal muscles and ribs.

(2) The Abdominal Muscles and their actions.

(3) The Diaphragm or the muscular partition between the chest cavity and the abdominal cavity.

(4) Respiration.

It is felt that this information can be of use for reference if necessary by the teacher or professor in demonstrating the breathing methods he advocates. In so doing it is advisable to exercise some care before making dogmatic statements to students regarding the rôle of certain muscles during playing. It will be seen that controversy exists not only among musicians (on such questions as the rôle of the larynx), but also among anatomists and physiologists (on such questions as the mechanical action of the individual intercostal muscles).

THE CHEST CAVITY OR THORAX

The chest cavity or thorax consists of a bony and cartilaginous cage which houses the lungs with the pleura, the heart with the pericardium, together with the trachea (wind-pipe), the bronchi, the œsophagus (gullet) and important blood vessels and nerves (see Fig. 31). In front it is bounded by the sternum (breastplate) together with the costal cartilages (the non-bony parts) of the first eight or nine ribs and the front bony ends of these ribs to which they are attached. Behind it is bounded by the bodies of the thoracic vertebræ (that is, the chest parts of the spine) and the spinal parts of the ribs as far as what are anatomically called their angles. Laterally, it is bounded by the ribs beyond their angles. The whole cage is barrel-shaped, is flattened from before backwards and is much narrower above than below.

The ribs (costæ) number twelve on each side. There are seven "true" ribs which articulate directly with the sternum through their costal cartilages and five "false" ribs, on each side. The first three of these have no direct articulation with the sternum through their own costal cartilages, but articulate with the costal cartilages immediately above. The last two ribs, i.e., the eleventh and twelfth, do not articulate with either the sternum or with the costal cartilages immediately above and are known as the "floating" or "free" ribs.

The Intercostal Muscles

These are usually described as two in number:

    (1) The External Intercostal muscle.
    (2) The Internal Intercostal muscle.

A third finer sheet of muscular fibres has been demonstrated which lies deep to both of the above (i.e., the intracostal or intercostal intima muscle) but with which we need not be concerned here.

    (1) The External Intercostal has its origin at the lower border of the upper rib of an "intercostal space" and is inserted into the outer margin of the upper border of the lower rib of the intercostal space. The fibres are directed downwards and forwards. These muscles usually extend as far forwards as the junction of the bony or osseous portions of the ribs with their cartilages.

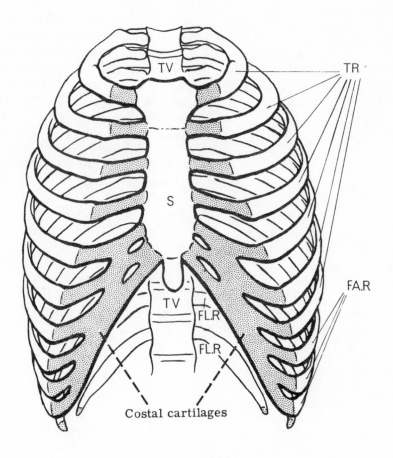

Fig. 31—The Thoracic Cage.

S, Sternum. TV, Thoracic vertebræ. TR, "True" ribs. FA.R, "False" ribs. FL.R, "Floating" ribs.

[*N.B.*—The darkened areas are the cartilaginous portions of the ribs (costal cartilages). The true and false ribs make a drooping curve outwards and downwards and forwards and upwards.]

(2) The Internal Intercostal has its origin at the upper margin of the costal groove of the upper rib and is inserted into the inner margin of the upper border of the lower rib. The fibres of this muscle are directed downwards and backwards. Each of the upper six muscles extend as far forward as the side of the sternum, thereby, unlike the external intercostal, having an interosseous (interbony) portion as well as an intercartilaginous portion (see Fig. 32). The external intercostal lies more superficial to the internal intercostal and the fibres of the former cross in the opposite direction. to the latter, i.e., at right angles to each other.

ACTION: The function of the intercostal muscles has been the subject of a great deal of investigation spread over a considerable period of time. Indeed, one eminent authority[21] states that "it has

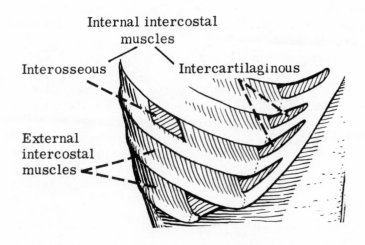

Fig. 32—The Intercostal muscles.

NOTE: (1) The external intercostal fibres are directed downwards and forwards and connect the bony (osseous) parts of the ribs as far as their junction with their cartilaginous parts. (2) The internal intercostal fibres are directed downwards and backwards but extend more to the front having interosseous and intercartilaginous parts.

been a source of controversy throughout medical history." Several conflicting theories have been held for centuries and according to the same authority "a detailed examination of each theory would be a work of scholasticism rather than of physiology."

The last statement can be well appreciated by the present author, who in seeking some early references, was impressed by the great detail in which the papers and theses were presented. Two of them,[22] from the middle of the eighteenth century, were in Latin. One attempted to prove his theory of the action of the individual intercostal muscles by means of intricate and lengthy arguments based on geometry and by mechanical models.

Some theories attribute certain opposing respiratory actions to the two individual groups of muscles, while other theories give the reverse actions to the same individual groups. Still others argue that both views are wrong and that the muscles work together in different movements of the chest during breathing. Some current standard anatomical works[23] state that while both intercostals are elevators of the ribs, they also form strong elastic supports which prevent the intercostal spaces being drawn in or bulged out during respiration.

Following a detailed and outstanding study of numerous investigations carried out, the eminent authority referred to above is of the opinion that one theory, Hamberger's,[24] is the most acceptable. It is that the external intercostals and the intercartilaginous internal intercostals raise the ribs and are therefore regarded as muscles of inspiration, while the interosseous internal intercostal muscles depress the ribs and are therefore muscles of expiration. He concludes, however, that the mechanical action of the individual intercostal muscles has not yet been fully established.

The Abdominal Muscles

The Abdominal Muscles involved in respiration are:

1. *The External Oblique*

This muscle arises from the outer surfaces of the lower eight ribs by means of eight slips. The upper five of these slips interdigitate with slips from the serratus anterior (see Fig. 33); the lower three with slips of the latissimus dorsi

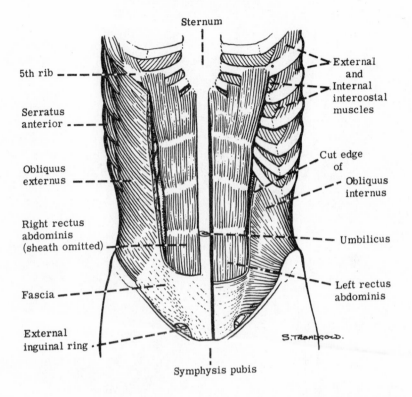

Sternum

5th rib

Serratus
anterior

Obliquus
externus

Right rectus
abdominis
(sheath omitted)

Fascia

External
inguinal ring

External
and
Internal
intercostal
muscles

Cut edge
of
Obliquus
internus

Umbilicus

Left rectus
abdominis

S. TREADGOLD.

Symphysis pubis

Fig. 33—To show the muscles of the abdominal wall and lower part of chest wall.
(The deepest muscle of the abdominal wall—the Transversus Abdominis—is here
excluded.)

NOTE: The muscles on subject's left are on deeper plane.

muscle. The fibres pass downwards and forwards, the
posterior ones to the iliac crest and the rest into a fibrous
aponeurosis which forms part of the sheath of the rectus
abdominis muscle (see below), blending in the mid-line with
its fellow of the opposite side. The lower border of this
aponeurosis forms the inguinal ligament.

2. *The Internal Oblique*
This muscle is on a deeper plane than the external oblique

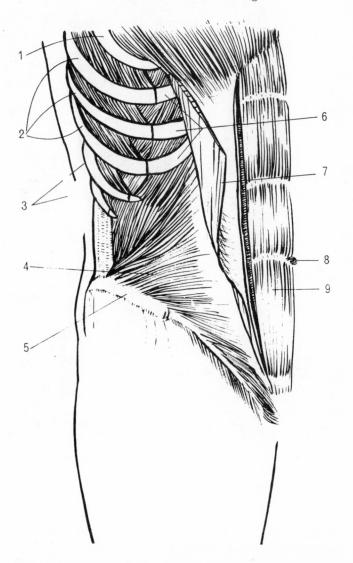

Fig. 34—To show direction of fibres of Internal Oblique Muscle of Abdomen (see text).
1. 7th rib (last "true" rib); 2. 8th, 9th and 10th ribs (upper three "false" ribs); 3. 11th and 12th ribs ("floating" or "free" ribs); 4. Int. oblique muscle; 5. Iliac crest; 6. Cartilaginous portions of 8th, 9th and 10th ribs; 7. External oblique muscle of abdomen (reflected); 8. Umbilicus; 9. Rectus abdominis muscle (sheath omitted.)

(see Fig. 34) and arises from the lateral half or more of the inguinal ligament, the iliac crest and the lumbar fascia.

The fibres pass upwards and forwards, and are inserted into the inferior edges of the cartilages of the last three ribs. The rest of the muscle passes fanwise over the side of the abdomen into the aponeurosis which forms part of the sheath of the rectus abdominis. It blends with its fellow of the opposite side in the linea alba, the lower part being inserted into the pubic crest.

3. *The Transversus Abdominis*

This muscle lies deep to the internal oblique and is attached to the deep surface of cartilages of the lower six ribs by fleshy slips *which interdigitate with slips of the diaphragm*. It is also attached to the lumbar fascia, the iliac crest and the lateral third of the inguinal ligament (see Fig. 35). Most of the fibres pass horizontally forwards and terminate in the anterior aponeurosis which lies behind the upper three-fourths of the rectus abdominis. It forms the deepest layer of the anterior wall of the sheath in the lower fourth of that

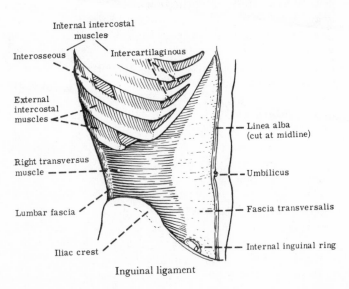

Fig. 35—To show the deepest muscle of the abdominal wall—the Transversus Abdominis.

muscle. The lowest of the lower fibres of the transversus abdominis incline downwards to arch over the spermatic cord in the male, or over the round ligament of the uterus in the female. It then terminates with the lower fibres of the posterior lamina of the internal oblique aponeurosis to form what is known as the conjoined tendon.

4. *The Rectus Abdominis*

This muscle arises below from the symphysis pubis and the pubic crest to be inserted above into the zyphoid process of the sternum, into the cartilage and bone of the fifth rib, and into the costal cartilages of the sixth and seventh ribs. With its fellow of the opposite side it forms two long vertical sheets of muscle, one on each side of the mid-line (the linea alba). At the junction of the lower two-fifths with the upper three-fifths of the linea alba is the umbilicus.

The Rectus muscle is enveloped over much of its length by the aponeuroses of the external and internal oblique and transversus muscles; this aponeurosis is referred to as the Sheath of the Rectus.

In its upper three-fourths the Sheath of the Rectus Abdominis is made up of two layers or laminæ in front and two behind the muscle. The superficial lamina is formed from the aponeurosis of the external oblique. The aponeurosis of the internal oblique splits to form one lamina in front of the rectus (deep to that of the external oblique), and another behind the rectus. Behind the latter is another lamina—that of the sheath which is formed by the anterior aponeurosis of the transversus abdominis.

In its lower fourth the Sheath of the Rectus Abdominis has three laminæ in front, formed respectively by the aponeuroses of external oblique, internal oblique and transversus abdominis. The sheath is deficient behind and is protected only by the fascia transversalis.

According to Dr. E. J. Moran Campbell[25] the abdominal muscles *as a group* have two important functions in respiration:

(1) Raising the intra-abdominal pressure.

(2) Drawing the lower ribs downwards and medially. The oblique muscles and the transversi are more important than the rectus abdominis.

A matter worthy of attention is that vigorous contraction of the abdominal muscles occurs in all voluntary expiratory manœuvres. Examples given are those of coughing and expulsion of reserve air. It might be that similar conditions occur in the wind musician during some musical passages. It would appear that the very high velocities of air flow which, it is suggested, occur during coughing, are dependent on the narrowing of the "tracheobronchial tree" (the air passages of the lower neck and upper chest) by a surrounding high intra-thoracic pressure. This in turn can be produced only by the contraction of the abdominal muscles. It would be analogous to the squeezing of a rubber tube through which air or water is flowing in order to increase the rate and pressure of flow. Similar conditions might equally apply in the case of the wind musician playing certain musical passages. It is of further interest that the transversus abdominis muscle, which is *active* during voluntary expiration, interdigitates (by the six fleshy slips mentioned above) with the rib attachments of the diaphragm—while the diaphragm itself is *passive* during voluntary expiration. This interdigitation may therefore account for the so-called "control of diaphragmatic action" which some wind instrumentalists claim to achieve during staccato playing (when the breath is being exhaled) and when the diaphragm is therefore necessarily passive.

The same fact—that is the interdigitation of the transversus abdominis muscle with the rib attachments of the diaphragm—might also be connected with, and perhaps partly account for what some eminent physiologists,[26] in a report on an investigation into expiratory pressures during speech and wind instrument playing, referred to as "puzzling diaphragmatic activity".

THE DIAPHRAGM

Separating the cavities of the chest and the abdomen is a large membraneous and muscular partition—the diaphragm (see Fig. 36). At rest it forms a double dome (see Fig. 37), the upper or convex surface of which is related on either side to the pleuræ with the lungs, and in the centre to the pericardium with the heart. The lower, concave, or abdominal surface is mostly lined with peritoneum and is related to the liver, stomach, pancreas and the kidneys (see Fig. 38). Its circumference is attached to the sternum in front, to the ribs at the sides and to the lumbar vertebræ behind and at a lower level (see Fig. 39). Its attachments interdigitate, at the cartilages of the lower six ribs, with the transversus abdominis muscle. The fibres are all arched upwards and inwards into what is known as the central tendon. There are three main openings, one for a very large artery, the aorta, which carries blood from the heart, another for a very large vein, the inferior vena cava, which carries blood to the heart and one for the œsophagus, which carries food to the stomach.

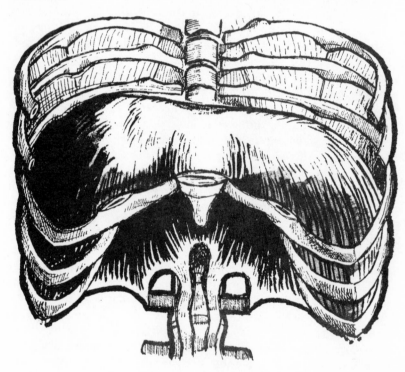

Fig. 36—To show upper (Thoracic) surface of Diaphragm.
NOTE: Sternum and parts of ribs excluded.

[*Reproduced by kind permission of the Royal Life Saving Society and of Dr. W.D.W. Brooks, C.B.E., M.D., F.R.C.P., in whose article on respiration in the Society's Handbook on Life Saving this illustration appears.*]

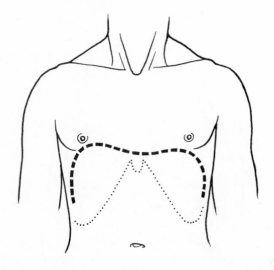

Fig. 37—Diaphragm. Surface outline showing "double" dome, in an approximate position.

When the diaphragm contracts, the dome descends and the base of the thorax expands. It also increases the vertical diameter of each half of the thorax. Its contraction elevates the lower ribs except the last (see Fig. 40A). The diaphragm is regarded as probably the most important muscle of inspiration.[27] When the dome descends the chest expands, air is drawn into the lungs and the abdominal viscera, related to its under surface, are displaced. When the diaphragm relaxes it recoils into its higher domed position in a purely passive manner. This occurs during expiration and when expiration is deep, largely due to the increased activity of the abdominal muscles, the diaphragm is passively forced upwards (see Fig. 40B).

According to an eminent physiologist,[28] the dome of the diaphragm, as seen radiologically, moves about 1.5cm. during quiet breathing and about 6–10cm. during a maximum breath (depending on the reference level for the measurement). The thoracic cavity is airtight and the wall within is lined with one of the two layers of pleuræ (parietal layer). The other layer

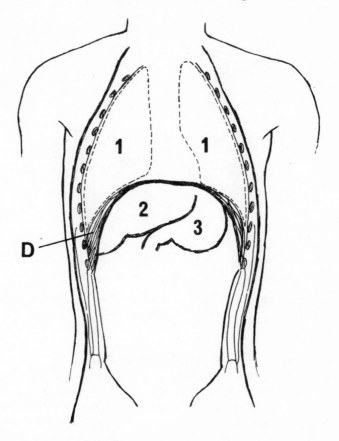

Fig. 38—Diaphragm. Imaginary section (coronal) through chest and abdomen
showing its high arch; its approximate relation to thoracic cage, ribs, pleuræ; and
its relation to abdomen, liver and stomach.
1. Pleuræ; 2. Liver; 3. Stomach; D, Diaphragm.

(pulmonary layer or visceral layer) covers each lung. Between
the two layers is the pleural cavity.

Air entering the mouth has no communication with the
pleural cavity. Penetration of the chest wall from without causes
collapse of the lungs. In certain conditions of disease, advantage
is sometimes taken of this in surgery to create an "artificial
pneumothorax",[29] in order to allow the lungs to rest and heal.

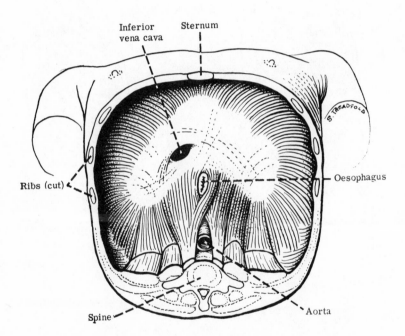

Fig. 39—To show inferior (abdominal) surface of Diaphragm.

Looking upward

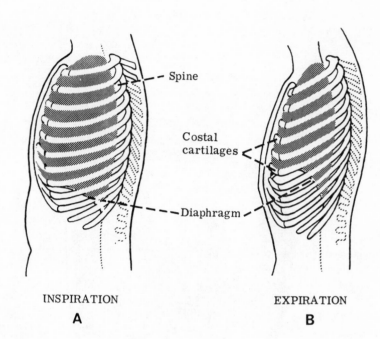

INSPIRATION
A

EXPIRATION
B

Fig. 40—To show movements of Diaphragm, Chest and Abdomen
during breathing.

A.—Deep Inspiration.

NOTE: (1) Descent and flattening of dome of diaphragm. (2) Lifting
of front of chest wall making ribs more horizontal. (3) Spine more
erect (slightly). (4) Relaxation of abdominal wall.

B.—Deep Expiration.

NOTE: (1) Raising of dome of diaphragm. (2) Dropping of front of
chest wall making ribs more slanted. (3) Spine more curved forwards
(slightly). (4) Contraction of abdominal wall (in voluntary or forced
expiration).

RESPIRATION

Briefly, this refers to the carriage of oxygen from the atmosphere to the cells of the body and the transfer of carbon dioxide from the cells back into the atmosphere.

The inflow and outflow of these gases to and from the lungs is referred to as *pulmonary ventilation*. The air passages are those of the nose, pharynx, larynx, trachea and bronchi. Within the lungs the bronchi subdivide until they reach their smallest branches which are called terminal bronchioles. Each of these contain a *vestibule*, off which are a number of chambers known as *atria*. These atria in turn communicate with *air-sacs*. It is as though the atria are irregular corridors, off which are rooms (air-sacs). The walls of the air-sacs are peppered with tiny *air-cells* or *alveoli*. The alveoli are the ultimate compartments in which gaseous exchange takes place between the inhaled air and the blood.

The blood vessels (arteries and veins) carrying blood to and from the lungs also subdivide into arterioles and venules becoming smaller and smaller until they reach the air-sacs, where the smallest arterioles connect with the smallest venules by what are called *capillaries*. A very close network of capillaries occupies the outside of the air-sacs. Such is the intimate connection between the air cavities and the capillaries that *diffusion* of gases readily takes place, e.g., between the oxygen in the inhaled atmospheric air and the carbon dioxide of the blood.

In quiet breathing there are two opposing acts:

   (1) Inspiration (Inhalation). This is said to be *active* and is due to the contraction of the muscles of ordinary inspiration and during this the thoracic cavity is enlarged in a healthy adult by about 500 c.c. This is known as the *tidal volume*. ⅓ liter

   (2) Expiration. The act of ordinary expiration is purely passive and is due mostly to the elasticity of the lungs and the chest wall. The amount of air expelled is the same tidal volume—500 c.c.

The *inspiratory reserve volume* is the amount of air that can be inspired *after* a normal inspiration. This amounts to about 3,000 c.c. in a healthy adult. The *expiratory reserve volume* is the amount of air that can be forcibly expired after an ordinary expiration and this is about 1,100 c.c. The *residual volume* is the amount of air that remains in the lungs after the most forceful expiration and this is about 1,200 c.c. The *vital capacity* is equal to the inspiratory reserve volume together with the tidal volume, plus the expiratory reserve volume, and this amounts to about 4,600 c.c. in a normal healthy male adult. In the healthy female adult the amounts are decreased by about 20 per cent. The figures are greater in larger athletic types than in the smaller less athletic types and are very approximate.

When breathing is carried out effortlessly it occurs normally about 16 to 18 times per minute. Of the inhaled air, only that part which undergoes gaseous exchange in the lung alveoli *each minute* is of significance for ventilation. Not all the air inhaled into the conducting pathways of the respiratory tract reaches the alveoli of the lungs. About 150 c.c. of this air remains in the upper respiratory tract of a normal adult. This part of the tract consists of the nasal passages, the pharynx, larynx, trachea and the bronchi and is called *The Dead Space*.

On exhalation, all the air in the dead space which did not reach the alveoli of the lungs is exhaled first, so that the amount of air which actually reaches the alveoli of the lungs is the tidal volume less the dead space volume. Furthermore, at the end of the exhalation the air that was in the dead space is now replaced with gas from the lungs which contains carbon dioxide. At the beginning of the next inhalation this gas in the dead space containing carbon dioxide enters the lungs before the inhaled fresh air. This is of much importance physiologically in a general way but it is of special importance to the wind musician, who is also voluntarily trying to adapt his depth, rate and pressure of breathing to conform with the requirements of his playing. For example, as stated above, normal quiet breathing occurs at about the rate of 16 to 18 times per minute. Should the same amount of air be inhaled by, say, twice the number of shallower breaths, the degree of alveolar ventilation is affected considerably. Since at each breath the dead space reduces the amount of fresh air reaching the alveoli of the lungs by about 150 c.c., it will follow that the greater the number of shallower breaths per minute, the greater the loss of fresh air per minute due to the dead space.

70

The sound of a wind instrument could be produced, theoretically, by air of any kind, whether fresh or expired, provided it is at the required pressure, since it is only necessary to generate the sound, which then resonates within the instrument. For example, in a pipe or reed organ atmospheric air is used. But in the wind musician, adequate pulmonary ventilation must take place and only the expired air can be used to play the instrument (except of course such instruments as the harmonica). The value of a selected kind of musical exercises where deep breathing is involved can be very considerable to the player. The intake of air, however, will need to be much more rapid to conform with the demand of the music, as well as with that of pulmonary ventilation.

Trained musicians learn how to control, within certain limits, the degree of pressure and the rate of flow of breath as well as the rate of inspiration or expiration. On certain occasions it might be necessary to utilize the whole of the Vital Capacity mentioned above, e.g., for a prolonged legato in crescendo or diminuendo. But it will be remembered that not all the energy expended in doing this is going to be converted into sound effect. There is a considerable wastage.[30] In order to vary the degree of breath pressure certain points of resistance in its path from the lungs to the instrument are used by the musician as well as the elastic recoil of the inflated chest and muscles of expiration. The air pathway from the lungs, as previously mentioned, is via the bronchioles, the bronchi and the trachea, via the larynx, oral pharynx and mouth and then past the lips.

It is in the larynx that the first "point" of resistance *can be made* to occur. The vocal cords are the means by which this is done. They can approximate together forming an almost closed slit, or they can separate widely. The opening between them is known as the Rima Glottidis (see Fig. 41). In speaking and singing the mechanism is more complicated than it may seem at first glance. For example, apart from the actual size of the larynx, or voice box, the edges of the cords which the exhaled air passes may be made thin and taut to increase the frequency of the sound emitted, as in soprano, or they may be thickened and made less taut as in bass. The variations in frequency in sound between these extremes may therefore be made consider-

71

THE LARYNGEAL CLEFT
During Deep Breathing

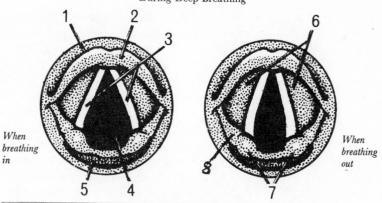

When breathing in

When breathing out

During Normal Breathing

During Phonation

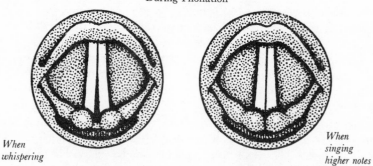

When whispering

When singing higher notes

Fig. 41—Scheme of Laryngeal Cleft (Rima Glottidis), as seen from above by laryngoscope, under different conditions.

1. Tongue; 2. Epiglottis; 3. Vocal folds ("true" vocal cords); 4. Rima glottidis; 5. Arytenoideus muscle; 6. Vestibular folds (false vocal cords); 7. Corniculate cartilage; 8. Cuneiform cartilage.

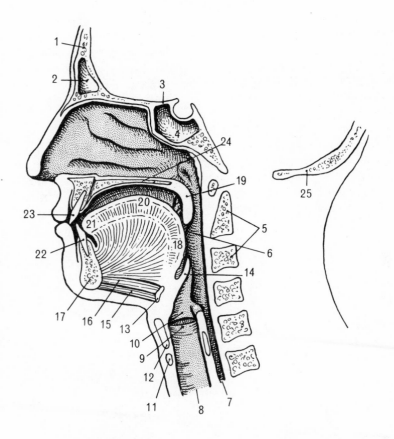

Fig. 42—Section (sagittal) through head and neck.

To show Air passages; auxiliary air cavities [excluding maxillary antrum (sinus) in side of nose (see Fig. 42A).]

1. Frontal bone; 2. Frontal sinus; 3. Sphenoid bone; 4. Sphenoidal sinus; 5. Cervical vertebræ; 6. Oropharyngeal isthmus; 7. Oesophagus; 8. Trachea; 9. Vocal folds (ventricular folds); 10. Vestibular folds; 11. Cricoid cartilage; 12. Thyroid cartilage; 13. Hyoid bone; 14. Epiglottis; 15. Digastric muscle (auterior belly); 16. Mylohyoid muscle; 17. Mandible; 18. Pharyngeal part of dorsum of tongue; 19. Soft palate; 20. Dorsum of tongue; 21. Tip of tongue; 22. Lower central incisor tooth; 23. Upper central incisor tooth; 24. Hard palate; 25. Occipital bone.

able, especially as this may be assisted by a complex muscular mechanism which may, for example, raise or lower the larynx. Furthermore, the *quality* in sound whatever the frequency, is then largely influenced by the organs and cavities of the throat, mouth, nose and head above the opening between the vocal cords of the larynx (see Figs. 42 and 42A). In these structures are most of the secrets of the individual's "supplementary resonance" discussed in the last chapter.

In order to appreciate more fully the rôle of the larynx in wind instrument playing a short account of this organ is given below. It is worth noting, however, that there is some conflict among wind musicians as to the extent of this "rôle".[31] Some appear to believe that it should have no part whatever in playing

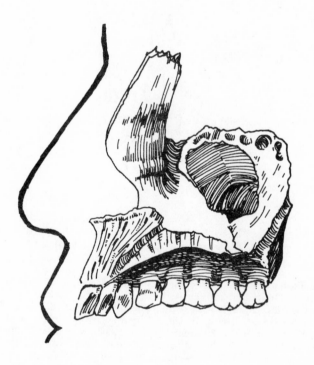

Fig. 42A—Maxillary sinus (antrum) in lateral wall of nose.
(*Not shown in Fig. 42.*)

a wind instrument, while others disagree. More agreement seems to exist in the fact that most teachers advise pupils to "imagine you are singing while playing". For any sound at all to emerge from the larynx, from a whisper upwards, the vocal cords must be made to vibrate by offering some resistance to the flow of breath.

THE LARYNX

The larynx is the upper part of the respiratory passage which is modified to form the organ of speech. Briefly, it is in the middle line of the neck, opening into the pharynx above and into the trachea below. It is provided with a complex of cartilages, joints, ligaments, intrinsic and extrinsic muscles and is lined with mucous membrane. There are nine cartilages, three of which are single, the other six being arranged in three pairs. The single ones are the epiglottis, the thyroid and cricoid. The pairs are the arytenoid, the corniculate and cuneiform.

The vocal folds (true vocal cords) extend to each side from the receding angle of the thyroid cartilage in front to the arytenoid cartilage behind. Above the vocal folds are two other folds of mucous membrane, more widely separated—the vestibular folds (false vocal cords) (see Fig. 42). Exhaled air, passing up from the lungs and trachea, has to pass through the larynx and here it can be intercepted by the vocal cords. At certain degrees of tension, when the exhaled air is forced past them, the cords will vibrate and this causes *phonation* (see Fig. 41). When the cords are sufficiently relaxed and the opening sufficiently wide phonation ceases and air passes through freely. During vibration, the elasticity of the vocal cords allows a little of the air column to force its way through, separating the edges. The edges are again approximated thereby interrupting the flow temporarily. When this is repeated at a rapid enough rate rhythmically, sound is emitted from the larynx[32].

An explanation appears wanting of the significance of the teacher's direction, advocated by some of the wind musicians mentioned above, to "imagine you are singing while playing" and to relate this to the rôle of the larynx. It is quite possible that the "unphonating" vocal cords might in some way, yet to be established by scientific investigation, be helping the generator (the reed or edge of hole in woodwind, and the lips in brass) to the extent that the sounds emitted during playing are "almost sung". The rôle of the larynx during wind instrument playing might be referred to, for want of a better expression, 'as "quasi-phonation" or as a "supplementary generator", or, as referred to elsewhere in this book, as a "supplementary resonator".

In *Brass* playing teachers often demonstrate the vibration of the lips without the mouthpiece. In so doing, they produce various "quasi-brass" tones at different frequencies, e.g., in the form of chords, octaves, arpeggios, and so forth. Often they are not aware, however, that they are causing the vocal cords to phonate at the same time, albeit in a whisper.

Without phonation of the vocal cords it would require a far greater head of breath pressure behind the lips to produce these "brass" tones clearly without the mouthpiece. A whistling sound can, of course, be produced by a smaller head of breath pressure. Nevertheless, the demonstration by the teacher is effective in impressing on the pupil that the lips do vibrate in order to generate the sound whilst playing. Even very quietly humming a tune requires the phonation of the vocal cords, however muffled or muted the sound might be. But for phonation not to occur and to "imagine you are singing while playing" suggests some sort of co-ordination of the vocal cords with playing. The rôle of the larynx might also be described as that of a "moderator" of the air column during playing. Whatever rôle the larynx might be proved to assume in wind instrument playing, it is, as stated before, in the larynx that the first "point" of resistance *can be made* to "occur".

The second "point" of resistance to the air column during exhalation is the approximation of the back of the tongue and the soft palate. The opening of the throat into the mouth where this occurs is known as the oropharyngeal isthmus (see Fig. 42). This is well known to all wind musicians in connection with articulation or staccato, such as in double or triple tonguing. The pronunciation of explosive sounds, such as "K" or "G" (pronounced hard, as in "good"), is caused by detaching the column of air with the back of the dorsum of the tongue and the back of the soft palate. Gutteral sounds are sometimes caused by the rhythmic vibration of the back edge of the soft palate with its uvula against the back of the tongue, both of which are in front of the exhaled air, which is at a certain head of pressure. In the field of jazz music certain spectacular effects are produced in wind instruments by such means.

The third "point" of resistance to the column of air is the top of the tongue below, with the hard palate above and the sides of the cheeks pressed inwards by the buccinator muscles (see Figs. 1, 2 and 3). Use of this "point" of resistance to the air column is best illustrated in "top-tonguing" ("dorsal-tonguing") or "soft" staccato and is produced by pronouncing the letter "D" or "N" or the sound "Th". Some individuals with easily controllable tongues can produce an acceptable rapid staccato by the rhythmic rolling of the letter "R" at this "point" of resistance.

The fourth "point" of resistance is at the tip of the tongue and its approximation with the upper front teeth on their palatal aspects, or with the front of the hard palate, or even with the inside of the lips (see Fig. 42). The action of the tip of the tongue, taking on, if necessary, the action of a valve, offers the best illustration of resistance to the exhaled column of air. Its use is of utmost importance to the wind musician in articulation—note "attack" and staccato in its "cleanest" forms.

The fifth "point" of resistance is at the aperture of the lips surrounding the air column. In brass playing the column has reached the "generator" of the instrumental sound, i.e., the lips, which will vibrate. In the flute the resistance of the lips diverts or directs the air column across the hole in the head of the instrument at a certain head of pressure. With the single reed instrument the lips, while acting primarily as a washer, will also allow the reed to vibrate at a required head of pressure. Each of the double reed instruments requires its own particular lip resistance to control the column of air which causes the reed to vibrate.

In all these "points" of resistance the modiolus of the embouchure (see Figs. 2 and 3) exerts an important part in control. It holds the muscles of the face, lips and most of those of the mouth in co-ordinated tension and balance. Whichever method of breath control might be advocated by a professor or teacher of a particular instrument, it would be well for him not to lose sight of the fact that the conditions in the physical make-up of different players may vary considerably and may be very different from his own. He is, understandably, often influenced by his own way of controlling his breathing and while attempting to pass this on for the benefit of his pupils, he may be liable to overlook these physical differences.

An important matter for the wind musician, particularly the teacher, to remember is that individual muscles seldom work alone. They almost always work as groups or complexes. On occasions a student is told to do something with *a certain muscle*. He is really working a group of muscles, although the work of an individual one might predominate, so that the object of the instruction might be achieved. Nevertheless, this is a case of what so often happens—namely, that the theory is wrong, but the practice is right.

To conclude this chapter, it will by now be apparent that the subject of the mechanical action of any of the muscles of respiration is a very advanced scientific study, even for a doctor. It demands a knowledgeable background of physiology and anatomy both in the laboratory and the clinic, and where this is lacking it should not be surprising if peculiar theories sometimes emerge. In my own study of the embouchure over several years, I was inevitably confronted with the related field of the study of breathing and the muscles involved. To understand this to the extent of passing on my knowledge of the embouchure, I had to, and was grateful to, draw on the knowledge of others—some of whom are world authorities in their respective spheres.

CHAPTER VI

THE EMBOUCHURE IN RELATION TO STACCATO

STACCATO: Detached or Separated. From *Staccare* (Italian)
to detach or to separate.

It is important to visualise that, before the beginning of a staccato passage, the column of air, which has already reached the "funnel-reservoir" of the mouth, is prevented from entering the instrument by the valve-like action of the tongue. At the beginning of the passage the air is released sharply into the mouthpiece by the equally sharp withdrawal of the tongue. The tongue would be withdrawn from the reed in reed instruments or from the palatal sides of the roots of the upper front teeth in all brass instruments and the flute and piccolo. (Withdrawal of the tongue from the lips in brass is strongly criticised by some authorities, while just as strongly advocated by others.) In addition, the column of air being forced up into the mouth by the elasticity of the lungs, and by the action of the abdominal muscles, and assisted by the plunger-like recoil of the diaphragm, is kept under restricted control within the mouth. The agent carrying out the control is a small area of embouchure musculature, under the necessary tension, *behind* the lips, near the corners of the mouth. To this small area—the modiolus—the tension is transmitted by the contraction of the muscles radiating from it. Should the passage of music continue in staccato, the tongue returns smartly, albeit gently, to its former position in order to repeat the process for as long as required. "Tonguing", in wind instrument playing is equivalent to "bowing" in violin playing.

The ability to produce a rapid staccato demands a very definite and acquired control of tongue movement and this ability varies considerably with different individuals. To some experienced players, particularly of the reed instruments, the control of the tongue during rapid staccato passages has always presented a problen which only a few seem to overcome to their own satisfaction. This sometimes gives rise to a certain lack of confidence in playing solo staccato passages. Some players find much difficulty in making the tongue respond quickly enough. To overcome the difficulty many subtle means of executing these passages are resorted to, such as modifying the phrasing into different grouping of the notes. Such devices are often used by some players with much artistry and musicianship. Their own interpretation will sometimes sound better than if they had adhered to the current written arrangement. It is possible that such arrangements could have been written by people with less experience of the wind instrument than the player himself. Be this as it may, it is nevertheless true that all wind musicians will admit, readily or reluctantly, that they admire the ability to perform perfectly a rapid and cleanly executed staccato. In view of the fact that some individuals are able to play any staccato passage with comparative ease, other players with some diffi- culty and still others with the greatest difficulty, it will be of advantage to explore the ways in which the tongue can carry out this important part of its work.

The foremost masters of wind instruments and most teachers seem to agree that the best staccato sound is produced by the part of the tongue nearest its tip.[33] For the tongue to execute such a staccato sound, however, it is dependent on many factors, some obvious and some not so obvious. These are its size, shape, muscular attachment to the jaws; its sensitivity, nerve supply, blood supply; the condition of its mucous membrane, the jaws, teeth, and so forth. It is agreed that in rapid staccato the with- drawal of the tongue's tip should be minimal, that is, the shortest possible distance back into the mouth before returning to its first position to be again withdrawn. Since most musicians are taught, in fingering their instruments, not to lift the fingers off the keys or pistons more than is absolutely necessary (in fact the fingers should hardly, if at all, leave the keys or pistons), the same principle might apply to the action of the tongue in rapid staccato, i.e., minimum of withdrawal of the tongue from the reed, lips, or palatal sides of the upper front teeth.

Perfect staccato, of course, demands perfect co-ordination of the releasing action of the tongue on the column of air with fingering of the particular instrument. Otherwise, on the one hand, control which is lost on the even detachment of the column of air, will tend to upset the embouchure musculature with resulting poor tone. Or on the other hand, it might throw the fingering out of gear, with resulting haphazard articulation of the musical passage altogether. Ideally, all the air of that part of the column intended to pass into the instrument by the valvular action of the tongue would be used for the purity of tone and staccato. But ideal conditions seldom exist, since lung ventilation has to proceed *pari passu* with playing. Furthermore, the breath expended during the effort in playing is mostly wasted in terms of actual sound produced, and some may in fact be lost intentionally through the side of the mouth. But should excessive air be lost unintentionally through the side of the mouth, control of tone, staccato and breathing would become correspondingly more complicated and sound effect more or less impaired. The force of the upward thrust of breath pressure from the lungs (by means of their own elasticity, that of the inflated chest and the action of the expiratory muscles), together with the degree of resistance offered by the embouchure musculature behind the lips and the muscles of the floor of the mouth and the side of the neck, will determine the intensity or "loudness" of the sound produced.

For the foregoing several reasons, careful phrasing needs intense practice in order to replenish breath through the corner of the mouth, or by dropping the lower jaw, as easily as one replenishes breath when pausing before continuing to speak or sing. However, in wind instrument playing breath intake must be of necessity very rapid and as silent as possible to escape the notice of the listener.

It was stated earlier that most of the foremost masters and teachers of wind instruments seem to agree that the best staccato sound is produced by the tip of the tongue. They are aware, no doubt, that to do this in a rapid manner for a comparatively long time is outside the capabilities of some otherwise fine musicians. Practice, of course, helps towards perfection, but for many it sooner or later becomes apparent that continued practice does not invariably achieve a perfect rapid staccato with the tip of the tongue. In these cases the teacher, having appreciated the pupil's difficulty, might well advise the careful practice of the alternative means of staccato production. Such means might eventually so closely approach the clarity of tip-tonguing as to be almost indistinguishable from it, yet sound equally pleasing. These alternative methods of tonguing are given later. To appreciate better the action of the tongue in wind instrument playing, a more detailed anatomical description of this organ becomes necessary.

THE TONGUE

The tongue is a large, very sensitive, mobile organ which, when the mouth is open, occupies its floor (see Fig. 43), and when the mouth is closed occupies almost the whole of the oral cavity (see Fig. 44), being in contact with the palate and teeth. It is composed chiefly of muscular tissue and is covered with mucous membrane. In the latter part of its structure reside the specific end-organs of the sense of taste, while due to the former, that is the muscular tissue with the special arrangement of its muscular fibres, it is capable of unique powers of mobility. It is thus well adapted to the normal functions of speech, taste, mastication and the swallowing of food (deglutition). Wind musicians attempt to train it, with varying degrees of success, to perform a valve-like function during playing, which is essential in articulation, note attack and staccato passages.

It consists of a root or base, a body and a tip.

The *root* is attached to the hyoid bone which is in front of the neck, just below the lower jaw.

The *body* consists of the bulk of the tongue as seen when the mouth is open and has upper and lower surfaces and right and left borders.

The *tip* is the front free extremity, which, when the mouth is in the rested position with the jaws practically closed together, lies behind the upper front teeth and is normally in contact with the front of the hard palate.

The top of the tongue is referred to as the *dorsum*. This is also free and when the mouth is closed it is in contact with the hard and soft palate. The front two-thirds of the dorsal surface, which is the oral part, and the top and sides of the tip are covered with a rough mucous membrane on which are distinguished several papillæ concerned with taste, while the back one-third is the pharyngeal part. The oral part and the pharyngeal part are separated by from 7 to 13 large papillæ (the vallate papillæ), arranged in the form of an inverted "V" and which deal with taste (bitter substances) (see Fig. 45). The tip and dorsum are involved in wind instrument playing.

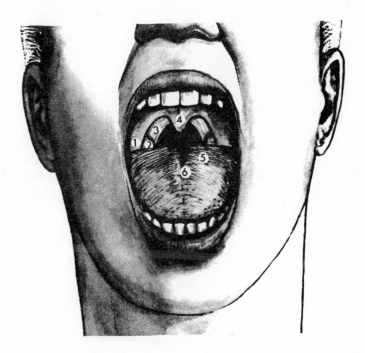

Fig. 43—The Tongue. At rest with mouth open.

1. Palatoglossus; 2. Tonsil; 3. Palato-pharyngeus;
4. Uvula; 5. Dorsum; 6. Median raphé.

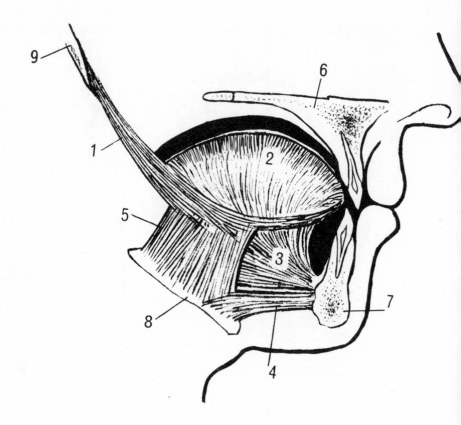

Fig. 44—The Tongue. At rest with mouth closed.

1. Styloglossus; 2. Dorsum; 3. Genioglossus; 4. Geniohyoid; 5. Hyoglossus; 6. Maxilla; 7. Mandible; 8. Hyoid
bone; 9. Styloid process of temporal bone.
NOTE: (1) Numbers 1–5 above are extrinsic muscles to
tongue. (2) Numbers 6–9 above are the bones to which
the tongue is attached (the maxilla indirectly, by means
of the palatoglossus shown in Fig. 43).

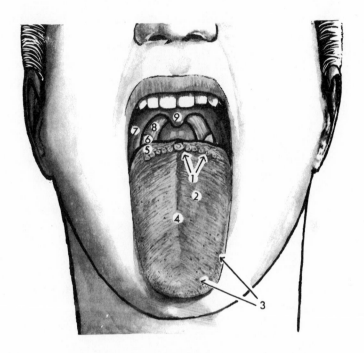

Fig. 45—The Tongue protruded.

1. Vallate papillæ; 2. Dorsum; 3. Fungiform papillæ; 4. Median raphé; 5. Lymphoid tissue; 6. Tonsil; 7. Palato-glossus; 8. Palato-pharyngeus; 9. Uvula.

NOTE: (1) The row of vallate papillæ deal with bitter substances in the sense of taste. This row marks the junction behind which is the pharyngeal part of the tongue. (2) Arranged in parallel rows from the median raphé outwards are closely set minute papillæ—the fili-form papillæ—which are the most numerous and give the tongue its frosted appearance. (3) The tip of the tongue deals with sweet substances in the sense of taste. (4) The lymphoid tissue at the back of the tongue is characteristic of the pharyngeal portion.

The muscles of the tongue are distinguished between (1) those which attach it to the bones outside the organ, i.e., the extrinsic muscles; and (2) those within the organ, i.e., the intrinsic muscles.

(1) THE EXTRINSIC MUSCLES

These are:

(i) The *genioglossus*, which attaches the tongue to the lower jaw behind and below the roots of the lower front teeth. ACTION:

    (a) All fibres acting together depress the tongue in the mid-line and create a furrow all along its length.

    (b) Acting singly, the posterior fibres protrude the tip while the anterior fibres retract the tip (see Fig. 44).

(ii) The *hyoglossus*. The fibres of this muscle arise from the greater horn of the hyoid bone and are inserted into the back half of the under surface of the tongue, near its side. ACTION:

    (a) Both sides acting together render the dorsum convex transversely and help to retract the tongue.

    (b) Acting singly depresses side of the tongue (see Fig. 44).

(iii) The *styloglossus*, which arises from a pencil-like projection of the temporal bone which is at the side of the head and base of the skull near the ear. Its fibres are inserted into the under surface and side of the tongue extending as far forward as the tip. ACTION:

    (a) Both sides acting together draw the tongue backwards and lift root of tongue.

    (b) Acting alone on each side draws the tongue to one side (e.g., tongue in cheek) (see Fig. 44).

(iv) The *palatoglossus*. This muscle arises from what is known as the palatine aponeurosis (a sort of flattened tendon) between the two folds of mucous membrane of the soft palate, which is attached in front to the back border of the hard palate and which becomes continuous behind with the aponeurosis of the pharynx.

Its fibres pass downwards and forwards to be inserted into the back part of the side of the tongue. Just behind it lies the tonsil.

ACTION:

    (a) To depress sides of the soft palate.

    (b) To draw the tongue upwards and backwards.

    (c) To draw the tongue and palate together as in pronouncing "K", "G" (see Fig. 43).

Many fibres of these extrinsic muscles of the tongue intermingle with the intrinsic muscle fibres. A point to note, which might be of some importance for wind musicians, is the relationship between the tongue through the styloglossus muscle with the temporal bone. This bone contains the external, middle and inner ear and the whole of the complicated mechanism which deals with hearing and sound analysis, as well as with equilibrium or balance.

(2) THE INTRINSIC MUSCLES (see Fig. 46)

These, as stated earlier, are contained entirely within the organ and consist of:

    (i) *the longitudinalis linguæ superior.* This is a flattened sheet of muscle fibres lying on the dorsum of the tongue under the mucous membrane and, as the name implies, extends longitudinally from the tip of the tongue to the body of the hyoid bone.

    (ii) *the longitudinalis linguæ inferior.* Takes the form of two rounded bundles of muscle fibres, one on each side of the under surface of the tongue. These bundles extend from the tip of the tongue backwards to the body of the hyoid bone. Behind, each lies between the hyoglossus on its outside and the genioglossus on its inside. In front it fuses with the styloglossus muscle.

    (iii) *the transversus linguæ* is a very thick layer of muscle fibres, which lies between the longitudinalis superior and inferior. The muscle on each side of the tongue arises from a fibrous partition between the two halves known as the *septum linguæ* and extends outwards. The upper fibres curve upwards to be inserted into the mucous membrane of the side of the tongue and the dorsum. This stratum of muscle is interspersed with fat

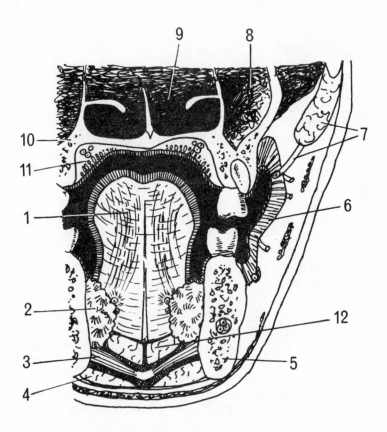

Fig. 46—The Tongue (coronal section). Showing its relationship to the cavities of the mouth, nose and face.

1. Intrinsic muscles of the tongue; 2. Sublingual gland; 3. Mylohyoid muscle; 4. Anterior belly of digastric muscle; 5. Mandible; 6. Buccinator muscle; 7. Parotid gland and its duct; 8. Maxillary sinus; 9. Cavity of nose; 10. Maxilla; 11. Palate; 12. Geniohyoid muscle. NOTE: (1) The tongue is covered on top with its mucous membrane, is doubly convex and is divided into two symmetrical halves by the septum linguæ. (2) The upper molar tooth is slightly outside the lower molar tooth.

and its fibres are broken up by fibres of the verticalis linguæ and the genioglossus.

(iv) *the verticalis linguæ.* The fibres of this muscle extend from the mucosa of the dorsum to the mucosa of the under surface of the tongue. The fibres are curved, with the convexities inwards, and decussate with the fibres of the transversus linguæ.

The septum linguæ is a fibrous partition which divides the tongue into two symmetrical halves and gives rise to the transversus linguæ on each side. It extends in the median line of the tongue from the tip to the body of the hyoid bone.

The extreme sensitivity of the tongue to the presence of foreign bodies or altered conditions is worthy of special mention, since it concerns all wind instrumentalists, perhaps the brass even more than the woodwind. For example, the presence of a hair may be definitely noticed by the tongue, even though it might avoid detection by the naked eye. Similarly, a rough edge to a recently damaged tooth (disturbances of a similar nature to the lips is dealt with later), becomes immediately noticeable. At best it can become a source of irritation to the tongue during playing; at worst it can give rise to much pain and upset playing. The tongue is immediately sensitive to any change in its usual environment, e.g., a new denture in the palate. It does, however, become adapted, albeit with some reluctance, but this takes some time and demands the perseverance of the individual. Particularly is this so with the wind musician.

TONGUING IN STACCATO

From the foregoing account, the action of the tongue in staccato might be conveniently subdivided into three distinct forms, for the purposes of teaching and description, as follows:

(1) That performed by the tip of the tongue, i.e., "tip-tonguing".

(2) That performed by the oral part of the dorsum (or top) of the tongue, which I propose to call "dorsal tonguing", or "top-tonguing".

(3) That performed by the pharyngeal or back part of the dorsum of the tongue, which I suggest calling "pharyngeal-tonguing", or alternatively "back-tonguing".

It will be noticed that both the "oral part" and the "pharyngeal part" refer to parts of the dorsum of the tongue in a strictly anatomical sense and in that sense accuracy in detail would seem to demand that tonguing should be divided into "tip-tonguing", "oral-tonguing" and "pharyngeal-tonguing". Now "oral" refers to "mouth" and a musician would hardly prefer to talk of "oral-tonguing", because all forms of tonguing are obviously carried out in the mouth. It seems to me that, from the musician's point of view, it is better and more descriptive to refer in an arbitrary way to tonguing with the tip ("tip-tonguing"), tonguing with the top ("dorsal-tonguing" or "top-tonguing") and tonguing with the back ("pharyngeal-tonguing" or "back-tonguing").

Tip-Tonguing

This gives the sharpest and cleanest form of staccato and is produced by pronouncing the letter "T" as in "TA" or "TU" or as "T" in combination with any convenient vowel sound—"A", "E", "I", "O" or "U".

In Reed Instruments

From an anatomical point of view the tip of the tongue refers to the front free end, while the wind musician usually refers to the "tip" of the tongue as being the very end or tip of this. The tip of the tongue leaves and returns to the tip of the reed sharply but as lightly as possible, in order to accent the note acutely. When applied to the first note of the staccato passage this can easily be achieved by all players. It is where this action of the tongue has to be repeated and kept up at varying speeds that the difficulty occurs, particularly where diminuendo or piano is to be observed. Here the musicianship of the player is put to the test. He might, with much subtlety, insert for all or some of the notes, except the first, a staccato effect produced by the letters "Te-de-te-de" or "The-de-the-de" or "The-ne-the-ne"; or he might practise so much, that he eventually achieves a "T" sound by pronouncing "Te-re-te-re" without letting the "r" roll out of control. All this depends on the way in which the front part of the base or root of the tongue is tied down to the lower jaw and the hyoid bone by the genioglossus and hyoglossus muscles. This varies about as much as faces and mouths vary.

The Embouchure in Relation to Staccato

IN BRASS INSTRUMENTS

Some controversy has for long existed as to the best way of producing the cleanest form of staccato sound. Some players have been taught that "it is best achieved by a sort of spitting lightly, as though a hair is being rid from the tip of the tongue, taking care that the tongue does not protrude beyond the teeth". This method is advocated by at least one of the finest exponents of the cornet in this country. Others teach that the tip of the tongue should touch the back of the upper front teeth near the roots. It should be remembered, however, that tongues, teeth and palates all *vary* in size, shape, etc. Therefore, it would behove teachers of any brass instrument not to dogmatise too much about exactly which part of the front of the tongue should touch which specific part of the front of the palate during a prolonged rapid staccato. It might be literally impossible for the pupil to carry out such an instruction, no matter how long he practised. The teacher might have found his own way comparatively easy, even when he started learning his instrument— for the very good reason that he was at a much better advantage regarding the size, shape, texture, flexibility and sensitivity of *his own tongue*, and the position and shape of his own teeth, jaws and palate. Therefore, it would perhaps be wiser, in the pupil's interest, to try to assess in the early lessons the pupil's capabilities of producing staccato, and to develop the best of them by supervised practice. In this respect it is the end result that matters rather than the way it is produced; e.g., the *sound* as it appears to the teacher.

In a general way tip-tonguing can be the means in brass wind instruments of playing a clean staccato by pronouncing the letter "T" as in "Ti-ti-ti" ("Tin") or in "Te-te-te" ("Ten") or in "Tu-tu-tu" ("Tuck") or in "The-the-the". Because of peculiarities in the form, shape and position of teeth in some players, it may be better to touch, very lightly, the back of the crowns of upper front teeth, instead of the roots in the palate. The crowns of the student's front teeth might be directed downwards and backwards, instead of downwards and forwards. In trying to carry out what the teacher himself does, the student might have to strain or shape his own tongue in a more complicated and tiring way.

Dorsal Tonguing (or Top-Tonguing)

The dorsum of the tongue is the top middle part, or most of what is seen of the organ when the mouth is opened and the tip is not lifted. It is convex from before backwards, while from side to side it is doubly convex, having a central longitudinal shallow groove or raphé (seam). This raphé corresponds to the dorsal part of the septum linguæ.

When a not too accentuated staccato is required this is the part of the tongue used, and such a staccato is best achieved by pronouncing the letter "D" as in "Da-da-da" or "De-de-de" or "Du-du-du". To do this the tongue misses the lips or the palatal aspects of the front upper teeth, but comes into contact with the front of the hard palate. The sound of "dorsal-tonguing" is not quite so explosive as that produced by "tip-tonguing". Where the individual has extraordinary control over rapid tongue movement in staccato, he is able to combine "tip-tonguing" and "dorsal-tonguing" with a remarkable amount of ease and with comparatively little practice. He detaches each note in a rapid passage by pronouncing "te-de-te-de" and practises this so that the sound of the "de" can hardly be distinguished from that of the "te".

It was mentioned above that the dorsum of the tongue is doubly convex from side to side and that in between, separating these convexities, was a longitudinal shallow groove corresponding to the median raphé (see Fig. 46). Now the column of air, which is thrust upwards into the mouth from the lungs, assisted by the diaphragm and intercostal muscles and the abdominal muscles, is guided along this furrow or groove in the tongue towards the mouthpiece of the instrument and the fore end of the furrow. It is then detached or chopped into its staccato sounds. In dorsal tonguing, the nearer to the fore end of the furrow the detachment of the air column takes place, the more it will sound like tip-tonguing.

Such an illusion is caused by a subtle and delicate co-ordination of three actions: that of the tongue with the diaphragm; that of dorsal-tonguing and that of tip-tonguing. The dorsum and tip of the tongue barely move back into the mouth before tilting slightly forwards again, in unison with an almost imperceptible upthrust of air, probably initiated by the action of the abdomen muscles. Should this upthrust be more than delicate these efforts will be found to be tiring in players of slight build, and the staccato will have a thumping sound, somewhat like a drum beat; the "beating of the diaphragmatic drum" due to the diaphragm being allowed to recoil into its higher domed position in short bursts.

It can be visualised that in front of the mouth the column of air passing through the funnel is bordered above by the palate, below by the median raphé of the dorsum of the tongue and on either side by the inner parts of the convexities of either side of the dorsum as well as the tensed buccinator muscle on each side. A very significant factor in influencing the shape of the tongue for this purpose is the embouchure musculature of the face, in particular the modiolus just behind the angles of the mouth on each side. When this is tense, the tongue tends to conform to the required shape, without alteration to tone quality.

It may seem strange, but in a fine player the more perfect all this adaptation becomes with experience, that is, the tenseness of the modiolus, the control of the co-ordination of the tongue movement with diaphragm action, the more the rest of the body posture, instrument balance and fingering, as well as attitude of mind, become relaxed. Moreover, placing the mouthpiece of the instrument on to a pre-adjusted embouchure to commence staccato becomes instantaneous and habitual with experience. Hence, it should not be surprising that any sudden alteration in any of these habitually co-ordinated factors can disturb the total embouchure balance.

THE PHARYNX (The Throat)

Briefly, this is a musculo-membraneous bag situated behind the nose, mouth and larynx. Above it is attached to the base of the skull; below it is continuous with the œsophagus or gullet. The nasal part and mouth or oral part are separated by the soft palate (see Fig. 42). The nasal pharynx is used for respiration only. The oral pharynx is mainly for deglutition or swallowing, but its front wall, which is the pharyngeal portion of the dorsum of the tongue, is also concerned with speech, e.g., in the production of explosive consonants such as K, or G, or of gutteral sounds. The laryngeal pharynx lies behind the larynx, and is also concerned with swallowing food.

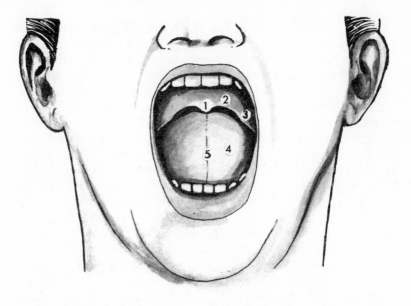

Fig. 47—The Tongue. Just before "pharyngeal-tonguing" ("back-tonguing").
1. Uvula; 2. Soft palate; 3. Palatoglossus muscle; 4. Dorsum; 5. Median raphé.
NOTE: Approximation of uvula and palate with top of back of tongue.

PHARYNGEAL TONGUING (or Back-Tonguing)

This is carried out by the back part of the dorsum of the tongue, which is anatomically referred to as the "posterior third". This part of the tongue, which curves backwards and downwards, is moved upwards smartly to shut off the passage of air into the mouth. At the same time the back of the palate (soft palate) and its small tongue-like projection which hangs down (the uvula) approximates downwards towards the tongue to shut off the passage of air (see Figs. 47 and 48). To operate this form of staccato the letter "K" as in "Key" or "G" as in "Get" is pronounced shortly and lightly.

Pharyngeal tonguing is generally used as an auxiliary form of tonguing where a very rapid rate of staccato appears in the musical passage, e.g., double-tonguing or triple-tonguing. Its use is common to all types of wind instruments whether brass or woodwind. It is often carried out in conjunction with tip-

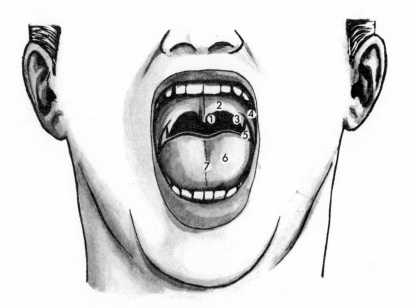

Fig. 48—The Tongue. Just after "pharyngeal-tonguing" ("back-tonguing")
1. Uvula; 2. Soft palate; 3. Palatopharyngeus; 4. Palatoglossus; 5. Tonsil.
6. Dorsum; 7. Median raphé.
NOTE: Separation of uvula, with soft palate, from tongue and vice versa.

tonguing or with dorsal-tonguing, or even with both. The syllables most frequently used are: (i) "Ti-ti-ki" or "Tikiti-kitiki"; or (ii) "Digidigi" or "Digidi-gidigi"; or (iii) "Tigigidi" or "Tidigi-tidigi". Variations of such combinations are performed within the capabilities of the individual players, the aim being to make the lightly explosive detachments as uniform as possible. On investigation of numerous experienced players, each seems to have his own pet way of producing the vowel sound. Some prefer "ah", some "oo" some "i" etc. Whichever is used, the ultimate musical staccato sound is the thing that matters. The ear of the player and listener is all important. Triple-tonguing and double-tonguing, to sound pleasant and appropriate, demand much practice of pharyngeal tonguing. Some players, particularly of the single reed instruments, are able to assist this form of tonguing with an acquired synchronising "passive action" of the diaphragm as with the dorsal tonguing mentioned earlier.

CHAPTER VII

THE EMBOUCHURE IN RELATION TO LEGATO

LEGATO: Bound or tied. From *Legare* (Italian)
to bind or to tie.

This instruction, given by the composer to the musician, is, according to some authorities[34], perhaps the most expressive in music. In creating his music, the composer has had the vision of these notes as being tied or bound together. The musician will at least attempt to interpret the instruction faithfully. Like all instructions, however, it can, of course, be ignored, but to ignore it would be unjust to the composer or arranger and might easily spoil the intended effect of the passage. It might also be a measure of the inefficiency or even inability of the player. Inability it might well be, when it is remembered that teachers of singing sometimes remind their pupils that "He who cannot bind, cannot sing".[35]

A *perfect* legato is not, however, possible on all types of instruments. It has been said that it is more than likely that a discriminating critic, if asked to name an instrument on which the ideal legato can be achieved, might well choose a wind instrument. Should this be so, a great responsibility would appear to fall on wind musicians, since for many of them it is by no means an easy matter to sustain legato throughout the whole compass of the instrument. That this is the case becomes obvious when two facts alone are considered. They are that wind instruments are generally very inefficient in terms of sound produced for energy expended; and that the rhythm of normal breathing can be interrupted or "controlled" only within certain limits since life itself depends on it.

Among wind players generally a great deal of time and effort is spent in practising staccato, a true rendering of which is most certainly a desirable accomplishment. The achieving of a true legato, however, requires an equal amount of patient practice, and, in the case of some instruments, even more. Apart from the required technique, both breath and tone in legato work have to be completely under the consciously controlled management of the player to obtain a desired effect. This he is only able to achieve by means of slowly training his breathing and embouchure musculature. Selected exercises with careful persistent practice, as so often stressed by the professor or teacher, will never be regretted.

Firstly, the player is able to train his lungs to store an adequate amount of air for the extended legato passage and to release it into the funnel-reservoir of his mouth at just the rate required, and with sufficient pressure for the whole of the passage. Secondly, he can train the modiolus on each side to a tension which makes the muscles radiating from it and the tongue resist and control the breath pressure from the funnel-reservoir cavity entering the instrument. As a result he will gain the desired tone colour and the required intensity of sound. Once satisfied with the result it can be persistently repeated, but it is unwise to do this to the point of exhaustion. An attempt is made to exert the maximum economy of breath expenditure. Deep breathing exercises would always be beneficial, but are not necessarily enough. Further advantage would be gained by practising with the instrument *rapid, deep inspirations*, followed by very slow and extended expirations. It will be found extremely difficult to accomplish this without a conspicuous hissing noise on air replenishment. While this noise should be minimised, it is far easier to do so in orchestral playing than in solo or concert work, due no doubt to the possibility of a certain amount of camouflage in orchestral playing.

A composer with a very good knowledge of wind instrument playing would be well aware of the breathing problems during long legato passages and would phrase the music accordingly for these instruments. Others not so well equipped would probably seek the advice of expert players or arrangers. A composer, however talented, with no such knowledge or without such advice, must then rely solely on the musicianship of the player, who would probably compromise between his own taste and the requirements of the conductor, as well as the composer.

Extended legato passages with inadequate intervals of rest can be much more tiring for wind instrument players than for those of string or percussion. The tiring involved here, in breathing, is additional to that caused by embouchure muscle fatigue and fingering, and is a matter not always given due consideration by some composers and conductors. Little excuse can justify the exhausting of wind instrument players unnecessarily unless the piece is deliberately intended to be a "marathon" where it would in any case be logical to allow for adequate rest periods in the music. The soloist or concert player, it will be remembered, has the additional ordeal of knowing that the attention of the audience is fixed on him and this tends to make him more easily breathless and to increase nervous strain.

It is worth remembering also, that all bodily activities can be tiring, so that should the wind musician know that a certain piece of music is going to put him to a severe test and strain his physical resources, he would be unwise to be extravagant with any physical movements, such as waving his instrument about needlessly. When the instrument moves unnecessarily during playing, the mouthpiece obviously moves with it and if the head of the player does not move at the same time, the embouchure must compensate in order to maintain tone colour and avoid loss of breath. This is all muscular effort and will take its toll in breath expenditure. Being at ease, whether sitting or standing, with fingers as near as possible to pistons or keys during playing, facilitates more rapid technique and minimises the muscular effort involved. Observance of all these facts tends to make the player more agile so that, while his mind concentrates on the music he is interpreting, the physical effort more easily copes with breathing, embouchure and fingering.

An extreme agility of tongue movement and its control is a great asset and can be acquired only after considerable practice. Working in close co-operation with the modiolus of the embouchure the tongue almost wraps itself under and on either side of the front of the column of air immediately before this passes into the instrument. The tongue is thereby furrowed along its dorsum towards the tip, thinning out or broadening the air column, tilting it into the mouthpiece or stretching it to the required length for the duration of the legato passage. At the same time, together with the modiolus, it influences tone colour.

The intensity of the sound is produced by the upthrust of air from the lungs by means of the plunger-like relaxing function of the diaphragm together with the muscular action of the chest wall and abdomen. All of these are aided by the relaxation of the muscles of the side of the neck and the floor of the mouth and by the precise resistance of the reed or lips. Without a well developed embouchure the lips become flaccid and much of the valuable air for the legato passage is wasted. Instead of passing into the instrument it is often lost through the corners of the mouth. Even where no breath appears to be lost it is worth remembering, as stated earlier, that wind instruments, from a purely scientific point of view, are startlingly inefficient in terms of energy used and sound produced. Therefore, if, added to this the sound producing mechanism of the player himself is not under complete control, his task is increased unnecessarily. This would apply to all the music he produces, but extended legato passages would particularly suffer.

Should the player be physically fit and his instrument the most responsive that he is able to obtain, and should the mouthpiece be the most comfortable and equally responsive, the most important remaining factor that will contribute to the best he can produce in sound effect would be his embouchure. The embouchure will be his "coupling" mechanism between his breathing apparatus and his instrument. It will help to control his air column, maintain his tone colour and co-ordinate his tongue with his fingers so that his musicianship is utterly unhindered in interpreting the composer's message.

Some legato passages might conceivably appear to be extended beyond the capability of lungs with the largest capacity, exerting the maximum economy. Here, the effect of the broken continuity of the passage depends entirely on the musicianship of the player. He takes as much advantage as possible of imperfections in the human hearing mechanism, and chooses to detach the passage at those points where it is least likely to be detected, at the same time rapidly replenishing sufficient breath to continue and complete the legato. Where the passage from one note to another is imperfect and where they cannot easily be bound together owing to the pecularities of the instrument—it is just at such points that again the musicianship of the player is put to the test. This breath replenishment should go practically unnoticed by the audience, particularly in a piano or diminuendo movement. Artistic phrasing, therefore, can be used to hide these peculiar imperfections in the instrument.

The economy of breath during legato might be likened to

pouring water from a kettle in a thin or thicker gentle stream. Coupled with the required variations in volume flow at any given moment it will be seen that a certain control in the tilting action of the kettle is necessary.

Similarly, during an extended legato passage economy in breath expenditure is carried out by a subtle co-ordination of the action of the muscles causing expiration of air from the lungs together with the embouchure musculature. Elsewhere the muscles are as relaxed as possible to allow free and easy movement for fingering and for the comfort of the rest of the body, while the mind concentrates on nothing but the music and its moods.

It will be apparent from all this how important it is for beginners and more mature students to carry out unfailingly the professor's or teacher's instructions to give adequate time to practising long notes in various shades of sound, e.g., uniform, crescendo and diminuendo as well as extended legato passages with similar shades. Thus legato playing on a wind instrument, every bit as much as staccato, is not only an important yardstick of the ability of the musician. It is also an indication of the state and development of his embouchure. It will tend to expose his weaknesses, whether his breathing is noticeably faulty, or whether his tone is colourless in various passages and out of accord with the moods of the music.

CHAPTER VIII

TIRING OF THE EMBOUCHURE MUSCULATURE

It is well-known that the muscles and nerves of the body which are put to work by our everyday conscious activities become fatigued and must be rested in order to be rejuvenated. For this reason we are compelled to spend about a third of our lives sleeping. This might be likened to the recharging of a battery in order to store more energy. Certain muscles and nerves, of course, never stop functioning throughout life, since life itself is dependent on the maintenance of such activity. Examples of such "essential services" are heart beat and circulation of blood, breathing and body metabolism. All the conscious bodily activities, such as work and play, are subordinate to these "essential services" and should not be continually excessive if a breakdown of the latter is to be avoided.

Normally, when the jaws are in a position of rest the mouth is closed or practically closed. In the absence of any conscious effort to keep it open, it will always tend to remain in, or return to, the closed, rested position. This is more readily seen if one considers the case of extending the arms out away from the body. Sooner or later the arms tire and tend to fall back to the position of rest near the body.

In blowing a wind instrument a conscious effort is used to keep the mouth open, however slightly. It is soon, however, working against the stimulus coming from the central nervous system, which is trying to close it. Since the muscles which are trying to keep the mouth open are weaker than the muscles which are trying to close it, they are fighting a losing battle, and so become more and more fatigued and the mouth slowly closes.

This may be termed from the musician's point of view "normal tiring" of the embouchure muscles. Where pain occurs in the lips it requires still *more* effort to keep the mouth open, however slightly, so that "rapid tiring" occurs.

To prove such a statement would be somewhat involved from a physiological point of view, but its truth may be illustrated simply in many ways. For instance, by running in a marathon an athlete would, inevitably, sooner or later become tired. But supposing he injured his foot badly, the added burden of bearing the pain would obviously make him tire more rapidly. Pain, whatever its cause, is nature's demand for rest. If rest is not forthcoming, not only may damage occur, but additional undesirable effects accrue, such as boredom, inability to concentrate, mental fatigue, and so on. For the wind musician, this could result in inefficient technique as well as deterioration in tone.

By heeding such indisputable facts the musician, teacher and pupil are able to learn how to maintain their maximum standard of playing for as long as possible. One way, for instance, is to attempt to eliminate any source of pain in the lips, or any other part of the embouchure apparatus. For example, where a tooth is missing, the sharp unguarded corners of the teeth near the space might cause "point pressure" on the lips sufficient to give rise to pain or discomfort. As playing proceeds this can become more and more painful and eventually unbearable. Some teachers, and also some players of the clarinet, who probably have rotated or sharp teeth themselves, state that the lower front teeth "should not cut into the lower lip"—and demonstrate their personal method of contracting the lower lip *against the front of the lower teeth* rather than over the cutting edges of those teeth. Unfortunately this creates "surface pressure", with the result that such front teeth are too often lost later (see Figs. 49 and 50). Early dental treatment such as splinting these teeth from behind would probably prevent their loss.

Muscular energy is supplied by oxygen in the air we breathe and by the metabolism of the food we eat. Fresh air and careful diet are therefore essential for maximum efficiency. It is far wiser and more beneficial to play or practise for short intervals frequently and regularly, rather than for exhaustingly long spells with comparatively long intervals of rest. It has been stated that one tremendous attack by an enemy with all the resources at his disposal can be overwhelming, while several attacks of less intensity might be resisted indefinitely. The question of the student's health, vigour and stamina can be a perplexing matter for the professor or teacher to consider. This is usually confidential between the student, his medical advisor and perhaps his parents, but in some circumstances it could be in the student's own interest if this confidence was shared with his professor or teacher,

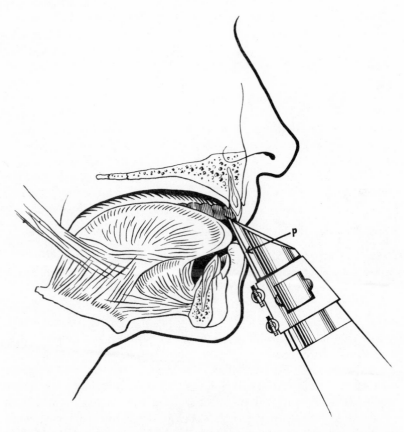

Fig. 49—"Surface-Pressure". Embouchure adapted to avoid "point-pressure" pain shown in Fig. 51.

NOTE: (1) Lower lip lying against front of crowns of lower incisors. (2) Compare with Fig. 51. (3) Instrument is more downwards nearer to body of player. (4) Crowns of teeth are pressed more inwards into mouth.

Fig. 50—To show tilting effect on Lower Front Teeth (due to embouchure adaptation as in Fig. 49).

NOTE: (1) "Surface-pressure" against front of crown of lower incisor. (2) Tilting effect in opposite direction of the apex of the root in the jaw. (3) Dotted tracing of tooth in its tilted position is purposely exaggerated to demonstrate the effect.

who would then be in a much better position to direct studies and assess progress.

It may well be that many illustrious masters of the past, composers and artists alike, might have bequeathed even more of their art to us, had they but heeded these harsh demands of nature. Where "rapid tiring" is seen to occur, say during blowing lessons, in an otherwise apparently healthy and robust pupil, it behoves the teacher to investigate the cause. Does the pupil play with his mouthpiece "dead-centre" or is he obviously "to one-side"? If he is "to one-side", the embouchure muscles are contracting unequally on both sides and for this to occur there must be some reason. It would help to find this reason, which might be purely psychological. Perhaps a habit is the cause, in which case this stands a good chance of being corrected with supervision. A more likely cause is that the pupil is un-

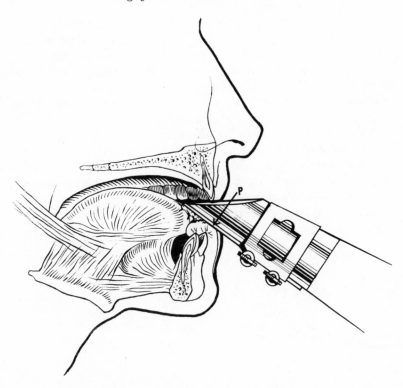

Fig. 51—"Point-Pressure". A common cause of pain in lip.

NOTE: (1) Lower lip curled over rotated incisor teeth in "single-lip" embouchure of clarinet player. (2) Upper incisor teeth pressing on upper sloping surface of mouthpiece causing lower lip to be compressed against rotated corners of lower teeth. P, "Point-pressure" on lower lip.

knowingly avoiding a sharp or damaged or rotated tooth which is hurting his lip (see Fig. 51). In a case like this the dentist's help might be considerable, particularly if he is made aware of the fact that his patient plays a wind instrument and if the patient takes his instrument with him when he is being dentally examined. Where the dentist himself plays a wind instrument, his help can be invaluable.

Although pain in one or both lips is the commonest cause of "rapid-tiring", it is not the sole cause. Decayed teeth, unerupted teeth, inflamed gums, ulcers on the mucous membrane of the tongue, lips or gums, might equally be the cause. Obstruction to embouchure adaptation to the mouthpiece caused by faulty fillings, crowns, bridgework, dentures, and so forth, might be the reason. In all these cases the dentist is in a position to help embouchure adaptation by smoothing sharp edges, redesigning fillings, crowns, bridges and dentures.

Tiring of the embouchure is therefore a matter which need not be considered lightly or treated solely as a matter of opinion, for, more often than not, slight physical conditions might be present which can be easily corrected. It is in the player's interest that they should not be ignored.

Conditions such as these, influencing the embouchure, will be considered in more detail in the next chapter.

CHAPTER IX

CARE OF THE EMBOUCHURE

Any student undertaking the arduous and lengthy task of becoming a professional wind musician is soon made aware of the priceless value of his embouchure and how much this depends on his lips, mouth, jaws and teeth. During his progress he becomes even more aware of this as he realises that the very sounds he produces and the promptness with which he is able to make them are going to influence his ability as a wind musician. As a musician he is forever eager to improve his embouchure and tries to eliminate any influence which hinders its development. Of the four factors mentioned above, by far the most likely to cause him trouble or anxiety later will be his teeth.

It has frequently surprised me considerably to learn how comparatively few wind musicians take meticulous care of their mouths and teeth. Endless hours are spent over the care given to their instruments, mouthpieces and reeds, with the object, of course, of improving playing and blowing with more comfort, as well as protecting the instrument itself. Such care is not misplaced, unless of course, it is allowed to become an obsession. It is obvious, however, that instruments, mouthpieces, reeds and such like, are all replaceable, however expensive and however difficult they may be to re-adapt to the musician's peculiar needs. The embouchure, it is equally obvious, cannot be replaced; and its care, as well as its development, needs all the meticulous attention the musician can give it.

Oral hygiene is of considerable importance to everybody, for the simple reason that so many of the diseases to which we are exposed, contagious or otherwise, gain entry through the mouth. The cleaner the mouth, the less likely it is to be affected.[36] The commonest diseases occurring in the mouth are those involving the teeth, their attachments to the jaws and the gums. All would be easier to cope with if pain were a guide, by acting as a warning. Unfortunately, this is comparatively rarely so. Some of the most hopelessly decayed teeth give no such warning sign. On the other hand some trivial carious cavities in teeth can give excruciating pain.

Most embouchure problems would be not nearly so common and difficult if the trouble were simply restricted to decayed cavities in the teeth. The collection of tartar or calculus on teeth frequently gives rise to a more insidious dental disease. For the average patient the loss of one or more teeth through neglect might be considered more or less serious; but for some musicians, especially the extremely nervous and sensitive types, it can be calamitous. The less sensitive individual would re-adapt his embouchure, should this be at all necessary, to a slightly different position and would probably play just as well, if not better, with the replacement of the missing tooth or teeth by a bridge or denture, as the case may be. The more nervous and sensitive musician has a marked tendency to panic. This is more noticeable among brass instrumentalists than any other, and is probably due to the dual function of the lips in brass playing (see Chapter I).

In an otherwise healthy mouth tartar normally collects on the teeth. The favourite sites are behind the lower front teeth and the sides of the upper back teeth (see openings of the salivary ducts below, Figs. 52 and 53). The tartar is usually quickly removed by making a routine twice-yearly visit to the dentist. A wind musician tends to secrete rather more saliva than other patients, since his playing would not tolerate a dry mouth for long. This in turn seems to accumulate more to the front of his mouth and probably results in more tartar formation.

Tartar, if left to collect, and this is usually due to an inefficient way of cleaning the teeth, burrows its way beneath the gum margin along the roots of the teeth. The gum is irritated by such constantly forming tartar and tries to "run away" from it. If the tartar is not removed, there comes a time when the gum can hardly move away any more and becomes swollen and inflamed. The first stage is what is known as a hyperæmia (loading up with blood) and the gums tend to bleed at the slightest touch. With further neglect the teeth may loosen in their sockets and pus begin to form. Such a condition is really the beginning of a destruction of the attachments of the teeth and although dentists prefer to avoid the term it is colloquially known as pyorrhœa. In the not so distant past such a condition would have meant

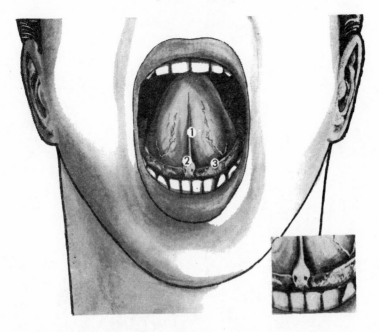

Fig. 52—Under Surface of Tongue.

1. Frenulum linguæ; 2. Papillary openings of submandibular ducts; 3. Raised ridges along which are minute openings of sublingual ducts (see text).

loss of most, if not all, the teeth affected and if the patient were a wind musician, denture problems of varying degrees of difficulty would have ensued.

In recent years considerable strides have been made in the dental treatment of these disorders (by means of clinical perio-dontology) and, with the co-operation of the patient, near-miracles have been performed on people in all walks of life, including wind musicians. However, prevention being far better than cure, in view of the discomfort, anxiety, time and expense involved, the wind musician would be very well advised to indulge in such a habit, or even fetish, of oral hygiene that any risk of loss of his teeth would be minimal over many years. Since the collection of tartar might be regarded as the initial stage of pyorrhœa, and since this is a deposit or precipitate from the saliva, it would not be amiss at this juncture to describe briefly

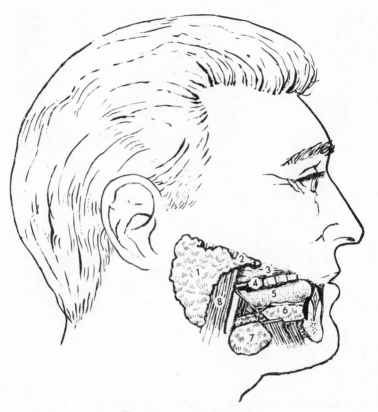

Fig. 53—The Salivary Glands.

1. Parotid gland; 2. Parotid duct; 3. Buccinator muscle; 4. Second upper molar tooth; 5. Tongue; 6. Sublingual gland; 7. Submandibular gland; 8. Masseter muscle.

how saliva, the secretion of the salivary glands, enters the mouth cavity.

By looking in a mirror with the aid of a bright source of light, compare Figure 52 with your own mouth, when the tip of the tongue is tilted upwards towards the palate. Two small pimples or papillæ will be noticed, one on each side of the mid-line near the floor of the mouth. These are the openings of two tubes or ducts leading from two glands under the sides of the lower jaw (mandible) near the angles. These glands are known as the *submandibular* glands and they pour saliva directly behind the lower front teeth. Along the raised ridges on the floor of the mouth which diverge backwards on either side under the tongue are minute almost invisible openings of other glands, one on each side, under the tongue and at the floor of the mouth. These are the *sublingual* glands. The sublingual (under tongue) glands are said to be almond shaped and together lie like the letter "V" converging towards the front behind the lower front teeth.

The largest of the salivary glands is the *parotid* gland (see Fig. 53). This is an irregular pear-shaped structure lying on each side of the face just in front of, and below, the opening into the ear, passing forwards over the large muscle (masseter) on the side of the lower jaw and downwards just above and behind the angle of the jaw. It also penetrates deeply and irregularly into the tissues behind the jaw and under the ear. This gland secretes or produces a more watery saliva than the other two glands which is passed by a duct or tube which opens through a flattened papilla located on the inside of the cheek at the side of the second molar tooth of the upper jaw. (The molars are the larger back teeth.) The favourite sites for the accumulation of tartar will be seen, for the above reasons, to be the back of the lower front teeth and the sides of the upper back teeth. In a badly neglected and dirty mouth, however, tartar will collect on most of the teeth.

The *Saliva* is a colourless viscid fluid secretion which contains many salts. These are said to be "in solution". It passes, from the glands, via the ducts and their papillary openings, into the mouth and for various reasons soon deposits or precipitates some of its salts in the form of calculus (tartar) around the nearest hard tissues—the teeth. It is well known that certain solids will dissolve in liquids to a greater extent when heated. Conversely, these salts will be deposited or precipitated when the solution cools. Tartar may be likened to the "fur" which collects in a kettle, especially in "hard" water districts. The salts in the water (lime) are held in solution during the heating of the kettle of water and are precipitated or deposited when the water in the kettle cools. The collection accumulates when more water is boiled frequently in the kettle and, if not removed, becomes a thick mass of "fur". It should be quite apparent now that if the teeth are not cleaned, or not cleaned well enough, tartar will keep on collecting with the formation of "pockets" between the gums and teeth and with the possible inflammation and results described earlier. While this is important to everybody, its extreme importance to wind musicians should not need further emphasis.

Earlier it was stated that some embouchure problems can be caused also by carious or decayed teeth. Dental caries is known to be one of the most prevalent diseases of civilised mankind, and indeed may be one of the results of that very civilisation[37]. It occurs particularly among civilised communities and in the more domesticated animals. The actual scientific cause is as yet said to be unknown in spite of the immense amount of study and research carried out for many years. There is no doubt, however, that the quality of our diet and our eating habits play a very important part in the incidence of dental caries.

Animals (including man) in their natural environment eat food mainly in the way Nature provides it. The fibrous element and natural juices present in such food encourage vigorous function of the teeth and jaws, so that the latter become well cleaned naturally, well developed and therefore well adapted to environmental conditions. The more the diet becomes over-refined, the more the valuable natural element is altered or lost. The teeth and jaws have less work to do and as a result become less developed and weaker. The structure of the dental tissues, such as enamel and dentine, which have become weaker, are so altered as to be more readily attacked by dental caries. For example, cane sugar provided in the natural state could be harmless to the teeth, since it requires considerable mastication and promotes a copious flow of saliva, cleaning the teeth naturally. When, however, sugar is in the over-refined granulated crystalline form in which we are accustomed to consume it, it becomes a potent and insidious factor in dental decay. It produces harmful acids which dissolve the enamel at its weakest spots.

The harmful effects of having "sweets" in all the various forms are even more profound. Boiled sweets or candies are often brought into contact with the back teeth, between them and the cheek. There they slowly dissolve and it is quite possible that the enamel in those positions dissolves with them. By "sweets" or "candies" is meant not only the "boiled" variety, but also the soft, sticky "caramels" children and some adults are so fond of, as well as the still softer chocolates, biscuits (cookies), ice cream and even "soft" fruit drinks. All are sugars whether in the solid state or in solution.

In civilised communities, such as those in which most of us live, all would probably be not nearly so bad if the standard of dental and oral hygiene were very high. Unfortunately, this is not the rule. All kinds of food, besides the sugars mentioned above, tend to collect around and between the teeth and, if left, in the presence of the moisture and warmth of the mouth, ferment and produce acids which result in dental decay. The teeth should be well brushed (it is surprising how few people know how to clean their teeth efficiently) *after* each meal. No food or sweets should really be eaten between meals without cleaning again if decay is to be avoided.

Those who find it "impossible" to clean their teeth after the mid-day meal, should at least adhere to a strict routine of cleaning *after* breakfast and *last thing* at night in order to ensure that no residue of food is left to decompose. It is quite a waste of time cleaning teeth before breakfast, as far as prevention of dental decay is concerned, if the food debris following the meal is to remain in crevices around the teeth. This care should apply equally to dentures where these are worn. Both the teeth and the denture should be well cleaned after a meal. Where bridgework is worn this personal care should be carried out looking in a mirror and routine visits to the dentist should be made about three times yearly.

In brushing the teeth well, it is not a question of how *hard* they are brushed but the *way* in which the brush is manœuvred around the teeth. It is best to brush the teeth of each jaw separately, that is, with the upper and lower jaws separated and not clenched together. The bristles should pass from the gum margin towards the biting surfaces and not across the necks of the teeth. It is best done with the bristles *first facing the gum margin* around the necks (gingivæ) on the outside near the cheek, and using a combined upward and rotating movement of the brush towards the biting surfaces of the teeth (see Fig. 54A).

Such brushing should be carried out systematically around the whole mouth. One could conveniently start at, say, the lower

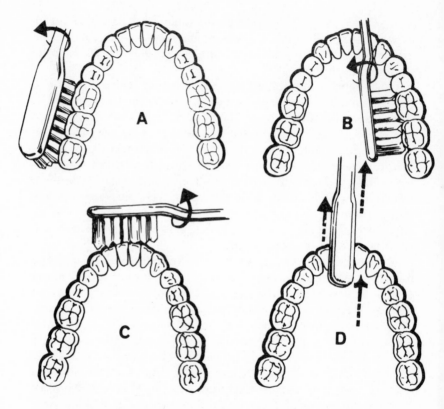

Fig. 54—Brushing the Teeth. A simple, efficient, systematic method: (A) Outside lower back teeth; (B) Inside lower back teeth; (C) Outside lower front teeth; (D) Inside lower front teeth.

NOTE: (1) Bristles of brush should *first face gum margins*. (2) Tops of back teeth are also brushed. (3) Strokes should be counted on each side and surface 7–10 times.

left back teeth on the cheek side, then the inner, tongue side (see Figs. 54A and B), then on the top surfaces, counting each time, say, 7 to 10 strokes. One can then proceed to the outside of the lower front teeth, starting with the bristles facing downwards on the gum, using a rotating upward movement towards the cutting edges of the teeth. Then the insides are brushed, this time with the brush held long-wise using an upward and outward stroke (see Figs. 54C and D). Having gone all round the lower jaw, the upper teeth are similarly brushed, this time from

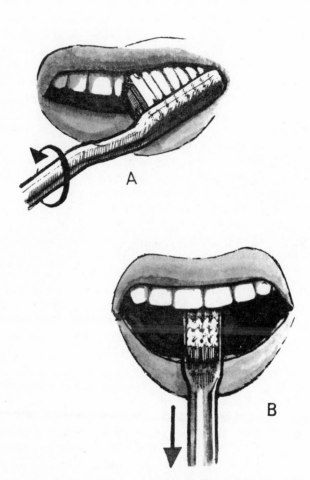

Fig. 55—Brushing the Teeth. (A) Outside upper front teeth: (B) Inside upper front teeth.

NOTE: (1) Bristles of brush in (A) should *first face upwards towards gum*. (2) Back teeth should be brushed outside, inside and on their top biting surfaces; in the first two cases with the bristles first facing upwards towards the gums. In every case 7–10 strokes are counted in order to clean all the teeth equally.

the gum downwards, counting in each area 7 to 10 strokes (see Figs. 55A and B).

The reason for counting is that a right-handed person is inclined to clean the left side more than the right, whereas a left-handed person nearly always brushes the right side more than the left. Counting helps to clean both sides of the mouth equally well. This whole systematic process of cleaning will be found to take hardly any longer than cleaning any other way or haphazardly. It has been found, in observing a large number of cases, that the average person takes approximately 10 seconds to brush his teeth! Such an astonishing fact can be verified by timing, watch in hand, another member of your own family without, of course, letting him or her know.

The type of toothpaste used is not of much significance, since most varieties today are very good. Some manufacturers, however, advertise the most extravagant claims for their products, such as killing the germs of dental decay within a few seconds, or the rapid dissolving of tartar and tobacco stains, and so on. Such claims are often misleading. For example, in the first case quoted, the germs, even if killed in a few seconds, are back again in another few seconds, because they are normally present in any healthy mouth! In the second case, any product that would rapidly dissolve tartar would most likely also remove some of the structure of the enamel.

The dental profession is of the opinion that a toothpaste is sufficiently good if it polishes the enamel, helps to remove food debris, is pleasant to use and has no abrasive or other harmful effect on the enamel and is not irritating to the soft tissues even if continually used. The type of toothbrush used is also important. Its shape, the type of bristles, handle, and so on, is a matter of opinion among dental surgeons. Most are agreed that a hard bristle can cause abrasion of the enamel near the necks of the teeth, where it thins out considerably, and recommend a soft or medium-soft brush whether animal bristle or nylon. Some dentists think that toothbrushes generally are far too hard. In the circumstances it would be best to use the type recommended by your own dental adviser.

In the opinion of the author, electric toothbrushes in the wrong hands can damage the enamel or soft tissues. On the other hand, intelligently used, an electric toothbrush can help to clean teeth efficiently, especially in awkward or otherwise inaccessible places. It is also probably useful for disabled or frail individuals.

Reference was made at the beginning of this chapter to the priceless value of the embouchure to the would-be professional wind musician. However, there are many hazards to which a musician's embouchure can be exposed, such as accidents involving jaw or facial injury, disease and so on. While in any other individual this is bad enough, he might, nevertheless, be in a position to continue to earn his livelihood after reasonable recovery. With the wind musician, it could be a much more protracted affair and occasionally a distressing impossibility. It is no use burying one's head in the sand and pretending that this might never happen. The plain fact is that it can, to the wind musician just as much as it can to anyone else. Car accidents, in particular, occur all the time.

Any means that would facilitate the conservation of one's embouchure apparatus and restore a damaged part to its original condition must be regarded as foresight and sound common-sense. For this reason the professional wind musician would be well advised to have his dental surgeon make artificial stone models of his upper and lower jaws and teeth, and even additional ones of his lips and mouth, so that these can be stored away in case of accident or other need. It might be an added precaution to have new ones made about every two years since the soft tissues change in contour, etc., and the teeth, in most cases, slowly change their position with time. Should any restoration be necessary by the dental surgeon or plastic surgeon following an accident or similar misfortune, obviously there is a much better chance of complete success.

There might be a note of profound pessimism in all this to some readers, but I do not consider the problems of the embouchure in this light. I look upon the problems as objectively as I can, where possible in a preventive way, to be compared perhaps with the way in which a doctor looks upon the problems of preventive medicine. Where prevention is not possible, then the best curative methods and aids available should be used.

This, to me, is sound commonsense.

CHAPTER X

CLEANLINESS OF INSTRUMENT

It was shown earlier that saliva deposits certain salts (tartar) around the teeth. It was also stated that a rather excessive amount of saliva gathers in the front of the mouth in wind instrument playing. The lips and tongue, moistened by the saliva, in turn moisten the mouthpiece; so that the viscid element of the saliva (mucin) settles there to dry into a layer of slowly increasing thickness. This layer incorporates within it numerous organisms. [38] It is obvious, therefore, that particular care should be taken to render the mouthpiece of the instrument as clean as possible as soon as a playing session finishes.

Passing an instrument, which has just been used by one player, to another player to blow, while quite a common practice, is a most unhygienic procedure and one which among certain people could arouse a good deal of justifiable repulsion. One of the players might have, or might be recently recovering from, a catarrhal infection, or something very much worse such as tuberculosis (which is not so common), or a gum disease such as Vincent's infection (which is more common). Should it be felt necessary on some occasions to pass an instrument in use from player to player, as when a teacher wishes to demonstrate an important blowing detail, or when an instrument is being tested before purchasing, some form of sterilization, while not perfect, is better than not observing any hygienic precautions at all. For instance, wiping the mouthpiece with spirit or some suitable antiseptic is a simple matter, so long as it is wiped dry with something clean, such as a disposable napkin, in order not to irritate the lips.

The benefit of such a practice on the teacher's part is to encourage in students and others a habit of hygienic care of their instruments on the one hand, while on the other promoting elementary cleanliness in his pupils. It might help against the contraction or spreading of a nasty disease. The author has on a few occasions seen a player wipe, with his soiled handkerchief, the mouthpiece of a clarinet which he had just been playing and pass the instrument to another player, who promptly put it into his own mouth. One would surely be shocked by the sight of a doctor or nurse putting a spatula, which had just been used for examining one patient's mouth, into the mouth of the next patient without sterilizing it. Although the chances of contamination might be small, the doctor or nurse would be the first to say that this is no excuse, because the possibility of contamination, however small, still exists.

Some players of wind instruments might wonder what connection there is between hygienic care of the instrument and the embouchure. It is simply this. Any easily cultivated habit which would directly or indirectly protect the embouchure from harm is a good habit. The author has known a few cases of players who had suffered varying degrees of incapacity with their embouchures and playing on account of debilitating mouth infections (including Vincent's infection mentioned above), some of which required prolonged treatment. These might conceivably have been caused by careless and unnecessary contamination.

It is quite likely that had the individuals referred to above given their instruments more hygienic care, they might have been spared such trouble with its consequent interference with health, work and finance. Hazards exist with almost every kind of occupation. Some are, of course, inevitable, but many are self-imposed as far as the wind musician is concerned and it would be nothing less than foolish of him to expose his health and earning capacity to any risks which could be avoided.

Any sort of mouth disorder or disease occurring in a very clean mouth stands a far better chance of responding rapidly to treatment than in a mouth which has been neglected. At the same time, there is far less chance of passing on such a disorder to another player or pupil. Similarly, a player with a very clean mouth has less chance of contracting such a disorder from another player by "mouthing" his instrument. For a pupil uninitiated in any hygiene procedures there is perhaps a little excuse. In a mature professional player, particularly a teacher or professor whose every action is likely to be emulated by the pupil, there can be no excuse.

In the use of any antiseptic, care should be taken to use a non-irritating kind in preference to a sharp, irritating kind. For example, spirit (or even brandy or whisky!) could be sufficiently effective, although not always completely, as this evaporates rapidly, leaving the mouthpiece cleaner and dry. Hence, it might be a useful suggestion to carry a small flask of spirit (or brandy or whisky) when conducting teaching lessons or tutorials. I sincerely trust such advice will not be misinterpretated!

CHAPTER XI

EMBOUCHURE AIDS

Detailed scientific studies of the playing of wind instruments have stimulated extraordinary efforts to solve the embouchure problems of many players. Outstanding among these efforts are those which have been carried out by the dental profession. Wind musicians at large will never know how much time and expense has been given to private research and painstaking experimental study, as well as laborious clinical investigation, into the problems of their embouchure troubles. Some of these troubles have been due to existing dental abnormalities, to diseases which could hardly have been avoided, to accidents, and lastly, but by no means least, to conditions due to sheer neglect on the part of the musicians themselves. Notable among the results which have emerged from dental research are Embouchure Aids.

To understand the purpose of these more fully it is necessary to explain briefly the difference between the individual teeth, the arrangement of the hard tissues from which they are constructed and how they are held within the jaws. Since the front teeth are the ones immediately concerned with the musician's embouchure comfort, the following explanation will be confined mainly to these:

In a normal human adult dentition there are 32 teeth: 8 incisors, 4 canines, 8 premolars and 12 molars in both jaws. In each jaw there are 4 incisors, 2 canines, 4 premolars and 6 molars, i.e., 16 teeth. On either side of the mid-line of the face and in each jaw there are 2 incisors, 1 canine, 2 premolars and 3 molars, i.e., 8 teeth. The incisors are chisel-shaped and are used for cutting or chiselling food; the one near the mid-line is called the *Central Incisor*, while the one to the side of this is called the *Lateral Incisor*. Next to the lateral incisor on each side of the jaw is the *Canine*, which is pointed and dog-like and is used for digging into, or tearing food. The *Premolars* and *Molars* are the back mangling teeth or grinders.

A typical front tooth consists of a "Crown", which is the part exposed into the mouth. This is covered with "Enamel", which is the hardest tissue in the body; it is thickest near the biting surface and thins steadily towards the neck of the tooth. The "Root" is that part of the tooth which is embedded in the bone of the jaw. The surface of the root is covered by a thin layer of hard tissue known as "Cement" or "Cementum". The bulk of the whole tooth which forms the crown and the root and which is covered with enamel and cementum is composed of "Dentine" or "Dentin". In the centre of the dentine and extending through the apex of the root is the pulp chamber and its pulp canal, or canals, which contain the "Pulp" or "Nerve". This gives nutriment and sensation to the tooth. The junction of the crown with the root is the "Neck" of the tooth.

The "Gum" is the soft tissue covering that part of the jaw bone surrounding the roots of the teeth, while the free ends of the gum surrounding the necks of the teeth are referred to as "Gingivæ". Separating the gingivæ from the neck of the tooth is the "Gingival Trough". It is in this trough that tartar often collects giving rise to "Gingivitis" and "Pyorrhœa". Separating the cementum of the root from the jawbone is the "Periodontal membrane", normally a thin layer of soft tissue fibres in which the tooth is slung in its socket in the jaw. It acts as a buffer or shock absorber during mastication, and gives pressure sensation to the tooth. Inflammation of the periodontal membrane or the pulp can give rise to the common "Dental abscess". On approaching adult life the enamel is substantially thick at the biting edges in the incisor teeth, but with the passage of time it is worn down by the action of the opposing upper and lower incisors. Such attrition tends to expose the softer dentine, so that there is unequal wear between the outer enamel and the dentine, giving rise more and more to a definite chisel form of tooth. The result is a sharp cutting edge on the *lip* side of the upper incisor and a similar sharp edge on the *tongue* side of the lower incisor (see Fig. 17).

It will now be seen that where the front teeth are in an even line there is a sweeping cutting line in the upper and lower front teeth and these can cause "linear pressure" on the lips giving discomfort or pain to players of reed instruments. Where the front teeth are in an irregular line, so that corners of the teeth jut on to the lips, the corners can give rise to even more discomfort or pain due to "point-pressure" (see Fig. 51). The discomfort can be in upper and lower lips where a "double-lip" embouchure is used, or it can be in the lower lip only where a "single-lip" embouchure is used.

Some players of single reed instruments attempt to avoid pain from point pressure by using an embouchure adaptation with the lower lip lying against the front of the crowns of the lower incisors rather than over the biting edges (see Fig. 49). Unfortunately, this method tends to tilt the lower incisors in their sockets (see Fig. 50), causing in time a mild inflammation which dissolves the bone around the roots and loosens the teeth. Should this occur and remain unnoticed or untreated, such teeth will almost invariably become very loose or be lost later. Where there is very slight linear or point sharpness against the lips, light stoning and smoothing of the enamel by the dental surgeon might be adequate to remove the discomfort or pain in playing. *On no account should this ever be attempted by the player himself.* The dentist knows just how much enamel can be safely removed, and this is very, very little indeed.

1. THE LIP SHIELD[39]

This is a thin layer of a suitable material, such as plastic, precious metal or even gutta-percha, which is moulded or cast to cover or blot out sharp corners or edges of teeth which would otherwise impinge on the lips during playing. It also obliterates uncomfortable spaces between teeth. Reed instrument players benefit considerably from the lip shield (see Fig. 56). Only in rare cases do brass players find them a help.

2. THE TOOTH SPLINT

This appliance can be made in the form of a removable skeleton, or as a fixture which embraces the palatal part of the crowns of the upper front teeth or the tongue sides of the crowns of the lower front teeth. Its purpose is to support the teeth from behind to prevent immediate movement of individual teeth, or to prevent "migration" over a long period. Brass players in particular benefit from this appliance especially where their front teeth have become loose.

3. THE EMBOUCHURE DENTURE

This is a special form of appliance made for players who have been unfortunate enough to lose all their natural teeth. It

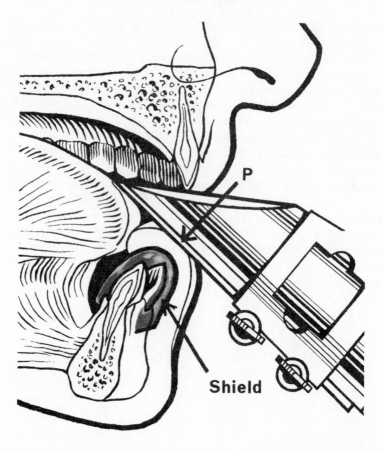

Fig. 56—The Lip Shield. This "embouchure aid" is intended to eliminate "point-pressure" or "linear-pressure" of the front teeth on to the lip. May be made (usually by a dental surgeon) for lower and/or upper teeth. Most effective for reed instrumentalists using "single-lip" or "double-lip" embouchures.

is designed solely to resist movement during playing and is not meant for any other purpose, such as eating. During playing, contact is maintained between the upper denture and lower denture on each side so that the top one does not drop and the lower one cannot be dislodged from the gum. Where a person has lost all his natural teeth and is already supplied with dentures, these are intended to fulfil the functions of eating and speaking as well as to restore the natural appearance.

The success of these depend not only on the ability of the dentist and the way they are constructed, but probably even more on the depth and condition of the gums which are to "hold" them. The latter vary considerably in different individuals. Some have even more gum than is necessary, while others do not have sufficient. Some people have hard and firm gums, others have soft and extremely tender gums, the tenderness being due to the sharp or irregular bone over which they are moulded. The longer the time that elapses following the extraction of teeth, the more the gums are absorbed or disappear. During mastication the teeth of each jaw function as a whole—broadly speaking, in an up and down movement and rather less from side to side or from back to front and *vice versa*, but always with the one jaw of teeth against the other. Added to all this, success also depends on the ability of the patient to persevere in using the dentures, and in some cases this might be the deciding factor. After all, if one has not sufficient patience or ability to learn to drive a car, however good a car it may be, one should not blame the car or the maker.

Now a person who has ample "hold" (or retention) for the dentures would probably be able to play an instrument quite well, while one with insufficient "hold" might find it quite impossible to play without dislodging them. It is these last cases which benefit most from the embouchure denture. There are some individuals who are very proud of the fact that they are able to play without either natural teeth or dentures. The reason for this is the simple fact that they have very deep and firm gums which have not entirely resorbed (shrunk), although they may also possess a better than average ability to withstand discomfort and so are able to re-adapt to a different embouchure. The vital fact however in these cases, is the possession of sufficient embouchure support.

In addition to embouchure aids, dentistry helps the wind musician in numerous other respects. Blowing may be made more comfortable by smoothing rough edges of teeth or fillings, or by the crowning of mutilated teeth. Routine dental "servicing" helps to maintain one of the most valuable assets of the wind musician, the "scaffolding" and "girders" of his embouchure mechanism. It helps to recognise, and prevent, future trouble and to keep the mouth clean and free from disease.

Sundry Aids

There are a number of other appliances which dental surgeons have made for individual cases which are ingeniously adapted to either dentures which are already worn or to natural teeth. The success of these depend not only on the ability of the dentist to design them, but also on their intelligent use by the player. There are still other "appliances" or "instruments", which might be regarded as aids: neck slings to assist in supporting the instrument; such helpful devices as the straightened crook and spike devised by Mr. William Waterhouse for the bassoon[40]; and shock absorbing inlays of rubber or similar material inserted into mouthpieces of single reed instruments. Well worthy of mention, too, are devices such as mouthpiece rim replicas on handles, advocated by some professors and teachers of brass instruments as aids in the practical study of individual embouchures. Professor Philip Farkas illustrates the use of these very well in his book *The Art of Brass Playing*. He also mentions the use of another piece of equipment—a small mirror, attached to the instrument lyre, which reflects the mouthpiece and embouchure of the player. Exact replicas of the rims of the player's own instrument mouthpiece could be made by his dental surgeon in various materials such as silver or chrome. And the dentist could also use such devices in locating and eliminating any adverse dental influences on the player's lips, particularly during the construction of crowns, bridge-work or dentures.

However, always make the dentist aware of the fact that you are a wind musician, as it is his primary job to make your mouth fit from a purely dental point of view, which is for eating comfort and speaking and to maintain a high standard, so far as he can, of your oral hygiene. Where a tooth or teeth have to be lost, or where a nerve is involved and has to be removed from the tooth, do not blame the dentist if you have allowed this to happen due to neglect or not keeping your regular routine appointments with him.

Finally, the best in the way of gold inlays, crowns, bridge-work or the most costly dentures is not too expensive, if you can afford them, so far as your embouchure demands are concerned. Instruments you can buy in plenty, in spite of your preference for only one, but you have only one embouchure mechanism. This you can possibly improve but rarely entirely replace.

CHAPTER XII

CONCLUSION

In this book I have tried to describe the musculature of the embouchure in its wider context—that is in its general operation in the playing of all kinds of wind instruments. In so far as I have succeeded the reader will have become aware of how intimately and how remotely this musculature becomes involved with breath control, with articulation and tongue control, and with resonance and its effect on tone colour. He will also appreciate more readily the importance of the peculiarities of any individual musculature (as applied to a single instrument) as well as that of the general embouchure requirements of different instruments.

Most players—and all teachers—of wind instruments will no doubt already be aware of some of the differences of embouchure adaptation to the same instrument by different players. But they may have been less aware of some of the more subtle influences on embouchure such as those of irregular teeth, gaps in the jaws and developmental defects in the jaws and lips. The intelligent appraisal of these factors, in which student and teacher can co-operate, can be invaluable in deciding the initial choice of instrument; and in this appraisal the advice of a dental surgeon can be very relevant. What I have said on the subject of embouchure potential and embouchure aids is, in particular, offered for consideration by teachers of wind instrument playing. It may also be of interest and use to composers and conductors.

So far as the embouchure of the player of an individual instrument is concerned, the subject of this book could well be explored in more detail in works devoted solely to the embouchure relevant to that instrument. That is, there could be works dealing exclusively with the embouchure of the oboe player, the player of the alto saxophone, of the flute, the tuba, the bass clarinet, etc. Some such works do already exist, but it would appear that much further anatomical and physiological research, preferably undertaken in co-operation with musical experts on the instrument in question, is necessary before the whole field can be authoritatively covered. It is for this reason that I have intentionally excluded from this book any special reference to such requirements as excursions of the lower jaw in the embouchure of certain wind instrumentalists. Such movements of the lower jaw vary not only with the different instruments but with the different types of faces and mouths.

As a musician the wind instrumentalist is a unique kind of executant. Like all other executants he uses his hands and fingers; as with the string instrumentalist, the fingering of a wind musician is by no means easy at any stage in his playing. In common with the singer the wind musician is all the time using his breath, his mouth, his lips and his tongue. The singer, however, is using an instrument which is built in to himself although the generator and resonator may need a long and intensive training before full control of them is achieved. In contrast, the generator and resonator of the music of the wind player are in his instrument, supplemented by some resonance within himself. But quite apart from these obvious factors which distinguish his playing from that of other musicians, there are others which should be taken into account.

During a working day of a maximum of some 16 hours (not including sleeping time) the mouth and its associated parts are normally occupied with eating, speaking and expressing emotion. Other than for these purposes hardly anyone uses his mouth, lips, tongue and jaws in such a precisely controlled, yet strained manner, for so many hours each day as the wind musician. Control must be precise for playing to be spontaneous, consistent and maintained. During eating and speaking precision is far less important. In eating it hardly matters whether chewing, for example, is carried out on one side of the mouth or the other or for how long it is carried out. Similarly in speaking, it is not imperative that speech should be carried out in any particular way. Since the playing of the wind musician must be, as I say, as precise as possible, certain habits must be deliberately acquired and deliberately developed. Moreover, the wind musician's breathing is compelled to function in the dual capacity of ventilating his lungs and blowing his instrument in a highly developed and controlled manner.

It is for these reasons that some wind musicians become extremely apprehensive and difficult patients for the dental surgeon. They are often obsessed, not so much with the possibility of pain, but with the possibility of a subsequent bad effect on their embouchure. Replacement of a tooth or teeth by a bridge or denture could easily necessitate some readjustment of the embouchure—an obviously disburbing situation to the wind musician who has already developed his embouchure. Nevertheless, some adjustment of embouchure adaptation by the player could, with a little patient practice, often overcome the problem completely. Indeed, in many cases the embouchure which appeared to be threatened could, in the event, actually end up as improved.

Problems regarding embouchure comfort have been discussed at some length. It only remains for me to add, in this respect, that lasting embouchure comfort could well depend on the care the musician himself gives to those structures on which his embouchure so much depends—his teeth, mouth and lips. Regular oral hygiene by himself and regular dental inspection (in his case about three times yearly) could be of paramount importance to the maintenance of his health and the security of his career and, in view of the hazards of tartar formation and dental decay, cannot be stressed too often.

Finally, I must state, for the peace of mind of many wind musicians (and possibly for the inspiration of a few) that there are some players who, while not being blessed by nature with anything approaching the near-perfect embouchure, and in fact having a variety of defects in their armamentaria, have nevertheless reached a very high standard of playing. While such achievements deserve the highest praise, and while they will no doubt be equalled in the future by other wind musicians who triumph over difficulties that those whom they surpass have not had to contend with, it is impossible not to regret that, in some cases, these difficulties were not reduced where they could have been. By that means, which is what this book is about, more good players could perhaps have been even better—and some of the outstanding ones, who achieved their excellence in spite of difficulties, might perhaps have achieved even more.

REFERENCES

1. De Peyer, Gervaise (1957) *The Wider View* in *The Woodwind Book*, pp. 80–85. Boosey and Hawkes; London.

2. Arban, J. B. (1953) *Cornet Method* (Parts I and II). Boosey and Hawkes; London.
   Blodgett, F. L. (1919) *Foundation to Trombone Playing*, p. 7. Carl Fischer Co.; New York.
   Camden, A. (1962) *Bassoon Technique*. Oxford University Press; London.
   Chapman, F. B. (1951) *Flute Technique*. Oxford University Press; London.
   Farkas, Philip (1962) *The Art of Brass Playing*. Brass Publications; Bloomington, Indiana.
   Rothwell, Evelyn (1953) *Oboe Technique*. Oxford University Press; London.
   Thurston, Frederick J. (1956) *Clarinet Technique*. Oxford University Press; London.

3. Campbell, E. J. M. (1958) *The Respiratory Muscles and the Mechanics of Breathing*. Lloyd-Luke (Medical Books) Ltd.; London.

4. Bennett, Sir Norman G. (1931) *The Science and Practice of Dental Surgery*. Vol. II; p. 758. Oxford University Press; London.

5. Thoma, Kurt H. (1946) *Oral Pathology*. Chapt. X; p. 488, *et seq*. Henry Kimpton; London.

6. *Ibid*. Chapt. XVII; p. 574.

7. Farkas, Philip *The Art of Brass Playing*. (See Ref. 2 above.) pp. 22, 23.

8. Fish, Sir E. W. (1948) *Principles of Full Denture Prosthesis*. Staples Press; London.

9. Lamp, C. J. and Epley, F. W. (1935) *Relation of Tooth Evenness to Performance on Brass and Woodwind Musical Instruments*. Journal of American Dental Association, pp. 22, 1232.

10. Handfield-Jones, R. M. and Porritt, Sir A. E. (1945) *The Essentials of Modern Surgery*. Chapt. XXI; p. 421. E. & S. Livingstone; London.

11. Langwill, Lyndesay G. (1965) *The Bassoon and Contra-Bassoon*. Chapt. II; pp. 161–162. Ernest Benn; London.

12. Porter, M. M. (Oct. 1953) *Dental Factors Adversely Influencing the Playing of Wind Instruments. The Role of Artificial Aids*. British Dental Journal; Vol. XCV, No. 7; pp. 152–160.

13. Reichenbach, E. and Brückl, H. (1936). Dtsch Zahnärtzl Wchschr; pp. 39, 213.

14. Arban, J. B. (1953) *Cornet Method*. Part I, p. 4. (See Ref. 2 above.)

15. Porter, M. M. (See Ref. 12 above.) p. 159.

16. *Ibid*. p. 154.

17. Bate, P. A. T. (1956) *The Oboe*, page 108. Ernest Benn; London.

18. Langwill, Lyndesay G. (See Ref. 11 above.) Chapt. IX; p. 145.

19. Berger, K. W. (1965) *Respiratory and Articulatory Factors in Wind Instrument Performance*. Journal of Applied Physiology (U.S.A.); Vol. 20, No. 6.

20. This account is based on the following works:
    Buchanan's *Manual of Anatomy*.
    Gray's *Anatomy*.
    Grant's *A Method of Anatomy*.
    Cunningham's *Text-book of Anatomy*.
    Jamieson's *Illustrations of Regional Anatomy*.
    Starling's *Principles of Human Physiology*.
    Samson Wright's *Applied Physiology*.
    Guyton's *Text-book of Medical Physiology*.

21. Campbell, E. J. M. (1958) *The Respiratory Muscles and the Mechanics of Breathing*. (See Ref. 3 above.)

22. Hamberger, G. E. (1749) *De Respirationis Mechanismo et Genuino Dissertio*. Li⊢rary of Royal Society of Medicine; London.
    Haller, A. (1758) *De Respiratione Experimenta* XII Francisci Grasset; Lausanne. Library of Royal Society of Medicine; London.

23. *e.g.* Buchanan's *Manual of Anatomy*, 7th Edition (1946). Balliere Tindall and Cox; London.
    Gray's *Anatomy*, 28th Edition (1942). Longmans Green; London.

24. Hamberger, G. E. (See Ref. 22 above.) pp. 1, 23.

25. Campbell, E. J. M. (1958) *The Respiratory Muscles and the Mechanics of Breathing*. (See Ref. 3 above.) p. 41.

26. Draper, M. H.; Ladefoged, P. and Whitteridge, D. (1960) *Expiratory Pressures and Air Flow During Speech*. British Medical Journal; No. 5189, p. 1843.

27. Gray's *Anatomy*, 28th Edition (1942). Longmans Green; London. p. 557.

28. Campbell, E. J. M. (1958) *The Respiratory Muscles and the Mechanics of Breathing*. (See Ref. 3 above.)

29. Handfield-Jones, R. M. and Porritt, Sir A. E. (1945) *The Essentials of Modern Surgery*. Chapt. XIV, p. 499.

30. Bouhuys, A. (1965) *Lung Volumes and Breathing Patterns in Wind Instrument Players*. Journal of Applied Physiology (U.S.A.)

31. Farkas, P. (1962). (See Ref. 2 above.) p. 62.

32. Rose, Arnold (1962) *The Singer and the Voice*. Ernest Benn; London.

33. Arban, J. B. (1953) (See Ref. 2 above.) Part I, p. 4; Part II, p. 188.

34. Kelsey, F. (During B.B.C. broadcast—*circa* 1951.)

35. Kelsey, F. (1950) *The Foundations of Singing*. Williams and Norgate; London. p. 116.

36. Bennett, Sir Norman (1931) *The Science and Practice of Dental Surgery*. Vol. 2, Chapt. XVIII, p. 759.

37. *Ibid.* Vol. 1, Chapt. XIII, p. 691.

38. Thoma, Kurt H. (See Ref. 5 above.) Chapt. X, p. 487.

39. Porter, M. M. (Oct. 1953), *Dental Factors Adversely Influencing the Playing of Wind Instruments. The Role of Artificial Aids*. British Dental Journal; Vol. XCV, No. 7, pp. 152–160.

40. Langwill, Lyndesay G. (See Ref. 11 above.) p. 160.

GLOSSARY

Abdomen	That part of the trunk below the diaphragm. Of uncertain origin, probably abdo—hide.
Adenoid	Glandular. Colloquially the plural refers to the lymphoid tissue at back of nose and throat (pharyngeal tonsils).
Alveolus	A hole; a little trough; the tooth socket.
Ansatz	"Setting on" (mouthpiece of wind instrument to lips).
Anterior	To the front.
Antrum	A cave or cavity.
Apex	Tip (e.g. of root of tooth).
Aponeurosis	An expansion from a tendon.
Arteriole	A very small artery.
Artery	Blood vessel carrying blood from heart.
Articular	Pertaining to a joint.
Articulation	Joint.
Arytenoid	Pitcher-like;—cartilage, cartilage of larynx.
Atrium	"Hall in a Roman house."
Attrition	dental, wearing down of teeth by mastication.
Biscuspid	—tooth, back tooth with two cusps.
Bronchiole	Small bronchus; branch of bronchus; air passage to and from lung.
Bronchus	*Lit.* pipe or draught; branch of wind pipe.
Bridge-work	Artificial dental appliance, fixed in mouth bridging a gap.
Buccal	Pertaining to the cheek.
Buccinator	*Lit.* a trumpeter. *Anat.* muscle of cheek.
Calculus	"Tartar"; "fur"; deposit on teeth.
Canine	—tooth, "dog-like".
Capillary	Tiny blood vessel uniting smallest arteriole with smallest venule.
Cardiac	Pertaining to the heart.
Caries	Decay.
Cartilage	Connective tissue, commonly referred to as "gristle"; tissue covering bones at joints, or between joints as articular discs. Tissue of which certain organs such as parts of ear, nose, larynx, etc., are composed.
Cementum (Cement)	Hard tissue surrounding root of tooth.
Central	Pertaining to centre;—incisor, large front upper tooth, or small front lower tooth.
Condyle	"Knuckle"; a rounded projection of bone covered with cartilage.
Congenital	Born with.
Corniculate	Horn-like;—cartilage, horn-like cartilage of larynx.
Coronal	Pertaining to a crown;—section, section as though through crown from side to side in vertical plane.
Costae	Ribs.
Costal	Pertaining to a rib.

Cricoid	Like a ring;—cartilage, ring-like cartilage of larynx.
Crown	—of tooth, part of tooth covered with enamel.
Cuneiform	Wedge-shaped;—cartilage, wedge-shaped cartilage of larynx.
Deciduous	Falling away;—tooth, "milk" tooth.
Deglutition	Act of swallowing.
Dentine (Dentin)	Hard tissue forming bulk of whole tooth.
Dentition	Arrangement and form of teeth and jaws.
Denture	Removable dental appliance bearing artificial tooth or teeth.
Diaphragm	Partition; *Anat.* muscular partition separating chest from abdomen.
Diastema	Space between two teeth.
Digastric	Having two bellies;—muscle, double bellied muscle, one from mastoid process to hyoid bone, other from hyoid bone to back of chin (front of mandible).
Distal	Towards the back.
Dorsal	Pertaining to the back.
Dorsum	The back;—of tongue, top (back) of tongue.
Duct	Tube; *Anat.* tube conveying secretion from a gland.
Einsatz	"Setting in"; form of embouchure adaptation.
Embouchure	See Definition, p. 7;—aid, appliance to assist embouchure comfort.
Enamel	Hard tissue covering crown of tooth.
Epiglottis	Leaf-shaped cartilage of larynx.
Eruption	—of teeth, "cutting" through gum; perforation of tooth through gum into position.
Exhalation	Breathing out.
Expiration	Breathing out.
Extra	Outside;—oral, outside mouth.
Extrinsic	—muscle, muscle outside the organ but connected with it.
Fascia	Bandage;—tissue covering muscles, etc., "like bandage".
Fatigue	—of muscle, tiring; physiological phenomenon due to over stimulation.
Fauces	Throat.
Fissure	A slit or cleft.
Flaccid	Limp or flabby.
Foramen	Aperture or hole.
Fossa	A ditch or trench.
Frenulum	A small bridle.
Frenum	A bridle.
Frontal	Pertaining to the forehead;—bone, bone of forehead.
Gastric	Pertaining to the stomach.
Generator	—of wind instruments, initial vibrator of air column.
Genio-	Pertaining to the chin;—glossus, muscle joining chin to tongue.
Gingiva	The free edge of gum surrounding neck of tooth.
Gland	Organ producing a secretion.

Glossus	Tongue.
Glottis	*Lit.* mouthpiece of a flute; *Anat.* trachea or windpipe.
Hyo-	Pertaining to the hyoid bone.
Hyoid	—bone, bone in front of neck, above "Adam's apple"; "wish-bone".
Hyoglossus	Muscle joining hyoid bone to tongue.
Hyper	Above;—too much.
Hyperæmia	"Too much" blood; "loaded up" with blood.
Hypo	Beneath, below;—calcified, under-calcified; not enough calcium; too soft.
Impulse	Physiological phenomenon relating to muscle and nerve.
Incisor	Cutter;—tooth, chisel-like front tooth.
Initiator	—of wind instrument, sound generator.
Inspiration	Inhalation; breathing in.
Inter	Between;—costal muscle, muscle between neighbouring ribs.
Interruptor	—of wind instruments, generator of sound; initial vibrator of air column.
Intrinsic	—muscle, muscle within the organ.
Labial	—surface of tooth towards the lip.
Laryngeal	Pertaining to larynx.
Larynx	"Voice-box"; organ of voice.
Lateral	To side;—incisor, front tooth to side of central incisor.
Levator	Muscle which elevates;—angular oris, muscle which lifts angle of mouth.
Linear	In a line.
Lingual	Towards the tongue; pertaining to tongue.
Longitudinalis	Muscle extending along length of organ.
Lymph	Body fluid conveying nutriment and carrying away waste products.
Lymphatic	Pertaining to lymph; sluggish (formerly attributed to "too much lymph").
Mandibular	Pertaining to the mandible.
Mandible	The lower jaw.
Masseter	—muscle, muscle of mastication.
Mastication	The act of chewing.
Maxilla	Upper jaw.
Maxillary	Pertaining to maxilla.
Membrane	Layer of soft tissue.
Mesial	Towards the mid-line.
Metabolism	The processes of biochemical change by which the cells of the body are kept alive. Food molecules are built up into higher complexes (Anabolism); complex molecules may be broken down (Katabolism); waste products may be eliminated (Excretion); gaseous metabolism is referred to as Respiration.
Modiolus	Nave of a wheel; centre point of union of muscles behind angle of mouth; meeting point of embouchure musculature; origin of orbicularis oris muscle (lips).

135

Molar	—tooth, large grinding or mangling tooth at back of mouth.
Mucin	Organic tenacious constituent of mucus.
Mucous	—membrane, lining membrane of body cavities having outlet externally.
Mucus	Fluid secreted by glands of mucous membranes.
Musculature	Term denoting system of muscles, e.g. of embouchure.
Occlusion	The act of closing the jaws with the back teeth clenched.
Oral	Pertaining to the mouth.
Oris	The mouth.
Orbicularis oris	Muscle surrounding the mouth (lips).
Orthodontia	The dental science and art of regulating the teeth, jaws and facial muscles; synonym—Orthodontics.
Palate.	Roof of mouth.
Palatal	Pertaining to palate.
Palatoglossus	Muscle joining palate to tongue.
Papilla	A small pimple.
Parotid	—gland, largest of salivary glands.
Periodontal	—membrane, membrane surrounding root of tooth, by which it is slung in its socket.
Periodontology	Dental science and art of preservation of teeth, gums and bone of jaws.
Pharynx	Throat.
Pharyngeal	Pertaining to the pharynx.
Phonate	To produce sound.
Phonation	The act of producing sound.
Pleura	The membrane lining the lung and inside of chest wall.
Posterior	The back.
Prime Mover	Generator of sound in wind instrument playing.
Process	*Anat.* projection (of bone).
Protrude	Jutting forward.
Prosthesis	The science and art of reproducing natural teeth by artificial means. Synonym—prosthetics.
Pulmonary	Pertaining to the lungs.
Pulp	Soft tissue (nerves and blood vessels) in centre of tooth.
Pyorrhœa	Pus in gums; a chronic inflammation of the gums and of the attachments of the teeth to the jaws.
Radiograph	X-ray negative to show internal structures.
Raphé	Seam.
Rectus	Straight;—abdominis, sheet of thin muscle stretching length of abdomen on either side of mid-line.
Reflex	Involuntary response to a nerve stimulus.
Resonance	Resounding (see Chapter 4).
Respiration	The intake of oxygen and elimination of carbon dioxide, and all the biochemical and biophysical actions involved.
Retrusion	—of lower jaw; lower jaw in abnormally backward position giving impression of protruding upper teeth.
Retention	—of denture. The ability of the appliance to withstand being dislodged. The support offered by the gums helping to retain the denture in position.

Risorius	—muscle, muscle of expression used in smiling and so forth.
Root	—of tooth, part within the socket of bone.
Sagittal	—section, section in plane down line from back to front.
Saliva	Secretion in mouth from salivary glands.
Septum	A fence or thin wall.
Sinus	A cavity or hollow.
Sternum	Breast plate in front of chest.
Sublingual	Under tongue.
Submandibular	Under mandible.
Supernumerary	Above the normal number.
Supplementary	—resonator, resonator within the air cavities of the head, neck and chest, which helps tone quality in wind instrument playing.
Stylo	Pencil-like.
Tartar	"Fur"—calcareous deposit on teeth.
Temporal	—bone, bone at side of head and face.
Thyroid	—cartilage, cartilage of larynx.
Thorax	The chest cage.
Tonsil	Gland on each side of the back of mouth.
Trachea	Windpipe.
Transversus	e.g.—linguæ, intrinsic muscle of tongue in transverse direction.
Ulcer	Sore lesion (wound) with bare raw surface.
Uvula	Tongue-like projection in mid-line of soft palate.
Vallate	—papillæ, large papillæ at back of tongue, each surrounded by a moat—deals with taste (bitter substances).
Vein	Blood vessel carrying blood towards heart.
Venule	Small vein.
Vertebræ	The bones of the spine.
Vincent's Infection	Infection of gums (gingivæ) causing ulceration and possibly destruction of gingivæ. (The germs involved can also infect the throat.)
Zygoma	Bone of cheek, shaped like a yoke.
Zyphoid	Sword-shaped—process, sword-shaped projection at lower end of sternum.

INDEX OF ILLUSTRATIONS

GENERAL INDEX

141

Jaw, jaws and teeth, function of, 8
  normal relationship of—and embouchure potential, 38
  "open-bite", 41, 43
  protrusion of lower—and embouchure potential, 40
  receding and protruding, 10
  receding lower—and embouchure potential, 38
  relationship to each other, 34, 35
  retruding lower, 20
  sunken upper, 19
  unequal development of, 41, 43
  "within the bounds of the normal", 22

Laryngeal cleft, approximation of, 71, 72
  Rima glottidis, 71, 72
  vocal cords in, 71, 72
Larynx, 75, 76
  role of, 74
  vocal folds of, 75
Latissimus dorsi muscle, 58, 59
Legato, 96–100
  and breath control, 97, 98
  diaphragm in, 98
  economy of muscular effort in, 98
Lips, function of, 8
  "Point pressure" of teeth on, 102, 105
  "surface pressure" of teeth on, 102–104
Lip shield, 123, 124
Lungs, action of, 8

Mandible, articulation of, 35
  diagram showing, 84
  movements of, 36, 37
Maxilla, non-movement of, 35
"Minimum-pressure system", see "Non-pressure system"

Modiolus, action of, 8
  control of air column by, 79
  definition of, 9
  in relation to embouchure musculature, 11, 12
  in staccato playing, 93
Mouth, action of, in guiding air, 8
  —breathing, 21
Mouthpiece, differing positions of, 9
  of different instruments in relation to embouchure, 7
  variations in, 24
Muscles, abdominal, 58–63
  external intercostal, 55
  internal intercostal, 55, 57

"Non-pressure" system, 24
  illustrated with cornet, 28

Oboe, embouchure where jaws, etc., are "normal", 18
  mouthpiece of, 7
  teeth irregularities and embouchure comfort in, 33

Pain, effect on embouchure of—see Tiring of the embouchure musculature
  unreliability of, as a warning of tooth decay, 107
Piccolo, mouthpiece of, 7
Palatoglossus, action of, 87
  diagram showing, 85
  position of, 86
Parotid gland, 110, 111
Pressure, between lower lip and teeth, 17
  see also "Non-pressure system"
Pharyngeal-tonguing in staccato, 89, 90, 94, 95
Pharynx, 93
Phonation, 75
"Point-pressure", 105, 122
  lip shield and, 124